THE COLOSSEUM BOOK OF CONTEMPORARY NARRATIVE VERSE

Colosseum Books

James Matthew Wilson, series editor

THE COLOSSEUM BOOK OF CONTEMPORARY NARRATIVE VERSE

Edited by Sunil Iyengar

FRANCISCAN UNIVERSITY PRESS

Franciscan University Press
1235 University Boulevard
Steubenville, OH 43952
740-283-3771

Distributed by:
The Catholic University of America Press
c/o HFS
P.O. Box 50370
Baltimore, MD 21211
800-537-5487

Cataloging-in-Publication Data available from
the Library of Congress

Cover and Interior Design by Reflective Book Design
Cover Image: Wirestock

Printed in the United States of America.

ISBN: 979-8-89372-119-5

Contents

Introduction ix

JARED CARTER (B. 1939) 1

Barn Siding 2

The Purpose of Poetry 21

BOB DYLAN (B. 1941) 22

Seven Curses 23

Lily, Rosemary and the Jack of Hearts 25

CHARLES MARTIN (B. 1942) 29

Passages from Friday 30

Coda: Mr. Dorrington's Discovery 51

B. H. FAIRCHILD (B. 1942) 53

Les Passages 54

MARILYN HACKER (B. 1942) 55

Vendanges 56

SYDNEY LEA (B. 1942) 60

The Feud 61

MARILYN NELSON (B. 1946) 76

The Ballad of Aunt Geneva 77

Freeman Field 79

ROBERT B. SHAW (B. 1947) 82
Birth of a Critical Spirit 83
Hide-and-Seek 85

DANIEL MARK EPSTEIN (B. 1948) 87
The Ferryman 88
Helen 90

MICHAEL DONAGHY (1954–2004) 91
Signifyin' Monkey 92
Black Ice and Rain 94

DANA GIOIA (B. 1950) 98
Counting the Children 99
Haunted 106
The Ballad of Jesús Ortiz 114

PAUL LAKE (1951–2022) 119
Inspectors 120
Walking Backward 124

RITA DOVE (B. 1952) 129
The Bistro Styx 130

ALBERTO RIOS (B. 1952) 133
True Story of the Pins 134
First Words 136
Refugio's Hair 137

GJERTRUD SCHNACKENBERG (B. 1953) 139
Two Tales of Clumsy 140
Darwin in 1881 144

MARY JO SALTER (B. 1954) 149

Frost at Midnight 150

DAVID MASON (B. 1954) 156

Gusev 157

Spooning 159

The Collector's Tale 165

PATRICIA SMITH (B. 1955) 174

Ethel's Sestina 175

Siblings 177

JOSEPH HARRISON (1957–2024) 178

Dickens on Fire 179

CATHERINE TUFARIELLO (B. 1963) 186

February 18, 1943 187

DAVID YEZZI (B. 1966) 189

Dirty Dan 190

Tomorrow & Tomorrow 194

CHRISTIAN WIMAN (B. 1966) 208

The Ice Storm 209

RACHEL WETZSTEON (1967–2009) 226

Madeleine for a While 227

A. E. STALLINGS (B. 1968) 229

Battle of Plataea: Aftermath 230

Lost and Found 233

JOSHUA MEHIGAN (B. 1969) 245

The Pig Roast 246

The Dream Job 247

The Orange Bottle 248

JAMES MATTHEW WILSON (B. 1975) 261

Bright Apples 262

The Great State of Alaska 264

PAISLEY REKDAL (B. 1979) 270

Philomela 271

ISABELLA HSU (B. 1996) 274

The Young Man at Nain 275

Acknowledgments 279

Index of Titles 281

Index of Poets 283

Introduction

This anthology assembles much of the best narrative verse written by American poets born since World War II. By offering selections from twenty-eight poets, it charts the revival and development of the short narrative poem over the past fifty years. To survey this body of work, spanning the last quarter of the twentieth century and the first quarter of the twenty-first, is to witness a quiet revolution in literary sensibility.

The oldest poets featured here began writing in the 1950s and 1960s. By then, a late Modernist consensus had privileged lyric poetry, licensing an array of specialized movements that critics branded accordingly. These trends included, among others, Confessionalism, Beat poetry, Deep Image poetry, the Black Mountain poets, the New York School, and Language poetry. Many of the resulting works have achieved canonical status. Many oppose the aesthetic ideals of Modernism itself. Yet, taken together, they have created a harsh climate for narrative poetry that is non-autobiographical in method and that follows one or more characters through a series of actions or events.

The poets in this anthology have recaptured storytelling for the art of verse. They often describe lives and situations radically different from their own. Like novelists, they work with imagined characters, scenes, and settings. Their poems, however, behave as short stories. In Aristotle's terms, each narrative has a beginning, a middle, and an end—though these may be scrambled when a tale requires it. But the stories also behave as poems, with every line and stanza earning its keep. Despite recent challenges to this form of writing, an ample fund of examples has accrued over the fifty-year period to enable a representative selection.

The sheer persistence of narrative poetry should not surprise us. As many ancient languages demonstrate, the practice of storytelling in verse is at least as venerable as the lyrical tradition. From the time of Homer, and even earlier, poets have not hesitated to shed their personal attributes and lose themselves in a crowd—or don the mask of another character entirely. Either mode can prevent poets from losing vital momentum when recounting, at length, an experience or observation. The poet not obsessed with self is better able to construct a milieu in which other voices and perspectives can be engaged, and in which a full sequence of actions can be related from cause to effect.

As a novelist, Virginia Woolf knew this instinctively. In "Letter to a Young Poet" (1932), she advised her correspondent, one John Leman, that to inhabit the lives of others would accelerate the learning of his craft:

> Two or three hundred years ago you [i.e., poets] were always writing about other people. Your pages were crammed with characters of the most opposite and various kinds—Hamlet, Cleopatra, Falstaff. Not only did we go to you for drama, and for the subtleties of human character, but we also went to you, incredible though this now seems, for laughter. You made us roar with laughter . . . .
>
> How can you learn to write if you write only about one single person? To take the obvious example. Can you doubt that the reason why Shakespeare knew every sound and syllable in the language and could do precisely what he liked with grammar and syntax, was that Hamlet, Falstaff and Cleopatra rushed him into this knowledge; that the lords, officers, dependants, murderers and common soldiers of the plays insisted that he should say exactly what they felt in the words expressing their feelings? It was they who taught him to write, not the begetter of the Sonnets. So that if you want to satisfy all those senses that rise in a swarm whenever we drop a poem among them—the reason, the imagination, the eyes, the ears, the palms of the hands and the soles of the feet, not to mention a million more that the psychologists have yet to name, *you will do well to embark upon a long poem in which people as unlike yourself as possible talk at the tops of their voices.* (italics mine)

To be asked to emulate Shakespeare is a daunting prescription for any would-be poet. A half century later, in an essay called "The Dilemma of the Long Poem" (1983), poet and critic Dana Gioia similarly called for greater range and versatility among the poets of his day. Yet, unlike Woolf, he counseled "a more modest aesthetic of the long poem" than before.

> American poetry needs … a less chauvinistic theory which does not vainly seek the great at the expense of the good and genuine. It needs to free poets from the burden of writing the definitive long poem and allow them to work in more manageable albeit limited genres like satire, comedy, unheroic autobiography, discursive writing, pure narrative—wherever, in short, their imagination takes them. It also needs to foster poems of "middle length," extended pieces not long enough to fill up an entire volume.

In view of his list of possible genres, there was nothing at all "modest" about Gioia's proposal. If they would only avoid conflating the long poem with the epic, he asserted, narrative poets could indulge all kinds of storytelling, both fiction and nonfiction.

A writer of Gioia's generation, David Mason, went so far as to claim, a few years on, that short narrative poems can be more effective than their prose equivalents. In an essay titled "Other Lives: On Shorter Narrative Poems" (1990), he said the poetic line "has advantages lacking in prose, the chief one being that it contributes to memorability, helping to sustain a literary culture most of us would agree is in danger of extinction." Story-poems, he continued, are at their most rewarding "in shorter narratives and monologues that can be read or recited in a single session."

Gioia and Mason were in the first wave of a host of writers who, beginning in the 1980s and 1990s, promoted traditional verse forms through their own examples and critical apparatus. Rhyme, meter, and fixed stanza patterns were embraced by this cohort, not only for lyric poems but also for long and short narrative ventures.

Many of these poets turn up in the following pages. Although fluency with formal verse techniques is not a criterion for entry, memorability is. To expand on Mason's paean to the poetic line: a full command of its metrical resources can be of distinct advantage to the narrative art. This much is clear from the survival of epics and ballads in the oral records of many cultures, where rhyme or meter—with or without music—served a mnemonic function. It is only to be expected, then, that most of the twenty-eight poets in this book should be skilled practitioners of formal verse.

Memorability, or the perceived capacity of a work to endure, is the sovereign rule guiding choices of narrative poem for this book. Another requirement is that the poem have attributes of a short story. The poem's speaker may be, and often is, a first-person narrator. But the narrator should not be readily identifiable as the poet *qua* poet. There are no personal memoirs, extended transcripts of a speaker's thought process, or explorations of a poet's identity.

Chronology is also a ruling factor. Although this volume covers a half century of American verse, the oldest poet in it was born in 1939. Excluded are the legions who came to maturity in the 1930s and 1940s, many of whom began to publish in the immediate postwar era. The choice to omit them was made to allow other, less anthologized poets to gain fresh recognition.

The 1980s and 1990s supplied the first generation of American poets self-consciously to advance narrative verse-writing. In those years, Vikram Seth, Frederick Turner, Robert McDowell, David Mason, and Mark Jarman published book-length poems in formal verse. (Seth is of Indian nationality, but he composed his Pushkinian verse novel, *The Golden Gate*, while enrolled as a graduate student at Stanford University.) In the first quarter of the twenty-first century, reinforcements came not only from the United States, but also from Canada and the United Kingdom. Book-length poems, not always in formal verse, issued from Anne Carson, Rita Dove, Robin Robertson, Glyn Maxwell, Jason Guriel, Aaron Poochigian, and, again David Mason. Over the same period, verse novels for children and youth reached unprecedented levels of popularity, earning prizes and sales.

These are all promising signs for the novel in verse—but what about the kind of narrative poem Gioia and Mason had called shorter or "middle length"? Such is the focus of the present volume, which, in consequence, carries no excerpts from book-length narratives, whether for children or adults. Instead, each entry is self-contained. All but one of the poets have an entry exceeding a page in length; roughly half the poets have an entry at least five pages long. These choices support a general proposition that the species of verse in greatest need of advocacy in our time is the mid-length narrative poem. It is a type not currently prominent in literary journals or in the few popular magazines that publish poetry.

The resulting selection shows astonishing range. Marilyn Hacker, Marilyn Nelson, and Catherine Tufariello narrate historical events concurrent with World War II. Alberto Rios, Gjertrud Schnackenberg, and Joshua Mehigan regale us with surreal or nonsense narratives. Charles Martin, Daniel Mark Epstein, A. E. Stallings, Paisley Rekdal, and Isabella Hsu recast episodes from literary classics, including works of ancient history, mythology, or Scripture. Other poets share gritty realist fiction (Jared Carter, Sydney Lea, and David Mason), literary biography (Schnackenberg, Mary Jo Salter, and Joseph Harrison), vignettes from film or theater (Rachel Wetzsteon and David Yezzi), and even one or two old-style Westerns (Bob Dylan and Dana Gioia).

In some poems the central action is slight. Examples are Epstein's "Helen," Dove's "The Bistro Styx," B. H. Fairchild's "Les Passages," and David Yezzi's "Dirty Dan." These entries, and both poems by Robert B. Shaw, qualify as an essential form of literary narrative: the anecdote. The Fairchild and Yezzi poems—along with Michael Donaghy's "Black Ice and Rain," Paul Lake's "Walking Backward," and Patricia Smith's "Ethel's Sestina"—may be classified alternatively as dramatic monologues. These demand inclusion because, in a hypnotic voice, each introduces a scene and then tracks the effects on one or more characters while an action unfolds.

To appreciate how signally the poets here have distinguished themselves from their peers, one has only to mark the atrophy of short narrative verse after Modernism. By 1942, Randall Jarrell was able to write of contemporary poetry that it was "essentially lyric: the rare narrative or expository poem is a half-fortuitous collocation of lyric details." In his 1928 essay "Is Verse a Dying Technique?" Edmund Wilson had argued that "the horizon and even the ambition of the contemporary writer of verse has narrowed with the specialization of the function of verse itself.... Would not D.H. Lawrence, for example, if he had lived a century earlier, probably have told his tales, as Byron and Crabbe did: in verse?"

The poets in this book have recovered for American verse some of the "horizon" and "ambition" of which Wilson spoke. Inevitably, their skills and techniques were enriched by the legacy of literary Modernism, and by the examples of other poets who had wrestled with it. But as writers of story-poems, they respond to a much older tradition.

For starters, between the fourteenth and eighteenth centuries, there had appeared such landmarks of English literature as *Piers Plowman, Sir Gawain and the Green Knight*, and various English and Scottish ballads. These centuries also yielded Chaucer's *The Canterbury Tales* (the true progenitor of many entries in this book), Shakespeare's two narrative poems, the great epics of Spenser and Milton, and mock-epics and epic translations by Dryden and Pope.

Even the rise of the novel during the eighteenth and nineteenth centuries failed to displace narrative verse. English Romanticism, a movement that in the popular imagination is often associated with self-expression and lyrical flights of fancy, coincided with one of the best periods on record for story-poems. Wordsworth's "The Ruined Cottage"; Coleridge's "The Rime of the Ancient Mariner" and "Christabel"; Blake's prophetic books; Burns's "Tam O'Shanter"; Scott's *Lady of the Lake*; Southey's epics; Crabbe's *The Borough*; Keats's "The Eve of St. Agnes," "Lamia," and "Isabella, or the Pot of Basil"; Byron's *Don Juan* and *Childe Harold's Pilgrimage*; and Shelley's "Julian and Maddalo" and "The Triumph of Life"—virtually each of these could be taken as a point of departure for succeeding generations of poets, and in many cases were.

For the remainder of the nineteenth century, substantial narrative verse arrived from both sides of the Atlantic. Tennyson, Poe, Longfellow, John Greenleaf Whittier, Elizabeth Barrett Browning, Robert Browning, Christina Rossetti, Matthew Arnold, Lewis Carroll, William Morris, and Robert Bridges all adopted the form. Poems such as Felicia Hemans's "Casabianca," Poe's "The Raven," Tennyson's "The Charge of the Light Brigade," and Longfellow's "Paul Revere's Ride" were assigned to schoolchildren for memorization. Newspapers also did their part: Ernest Thayer's comic ballad "Casey at the Bat" first appeared in the *San Francisco Examiner* in 1888. Two years later, Kipling's "Barrack-Room Ballads" began running in the *Scots Observer.*

Then, in the era directly preceding literary Modernism, narrative verse manifested in Oscar Wilde's book-length "Ballad of Reading Gaol" (1898) and in now neglected works, popular enough in their day, many of which reward reading: poems by Henry Newbolt, John Masefield, and Robert Service. In Scotland, Alfred Noyes's "The Highwayman" (1906), first published in *Blackwood's Magazine*, became an international hit. As with certain narratives by Tennyson, Longfellow, Poe, Kipling, and Service, this ballad was a popular recital piece. It was even adapted for Hollywood.

A few years later, in 1912, the English poet Walter de la Mare published *The Listener and Other Poems*. The title poem remains an anthology favorite. Also, though seldom read today, Stephen Vincent Benét, an American, turned out a sequence of book-length poems such as the Pulitzer Prize-winning *John Brown's Body* (1928) and, later in his brief life, apocalyptic or science-fiction narratives in short verse (e.g., "1936" and "Nightmare for Future Reference").

But it was an English novelist-poet who pioneered the type of narrative verse we would come to recognize in the twentieth century, on those increasingly rare occasions when story-poems appeared. Thomas Hardy, whose career straddled both the late Victorian and early Modernist phases, deposited short narrative poems in his collections, which otherwise swelled with lyrical offerings. Moreover, although he wrote an epic verse-and-prose drama, *The Dynasts*, which treated of the Napoleonic wars, his narrative poems recount far less momentous occasions—what one of his books (and a discrete section within it) calls, in the title, "satires of circumstance." The poems often concern disillusionment between lovers or the hauntings of remorse; they rely heavily on dialogue, as if he were composing a playlet on the slender basis of an anecdote or Sussex tale. *Time's Laughingstocks* (1909) is full of such poems.

Hardy introduced a mode that would dominate some of the most memorable narrative verse in the twentieth century. The poems are typically one to four pages; they display facility with a range of verse forms (sometimes invented for the occasion); they abound in naturalist evocations of people, speech, and actions in provincial settings; and they resolve in irresolution—which is to say that Hardy affirms the lyric's prerogative to ask questions but leave them unanswered. He thereby cleared space for two American realists—each, like him, a master of formal verse and a merciless chronicler of irony and self-delusion.

Edwin Arlington Robinson and Robert Frost ushered into the twentieth century a new age of American narrative verse, for those who would bid to follow. Among many other qualities setting apart the two poets from their respective generations is the large number of story-poems each produced. This feat invites comparisons with the subset of Romantic and Victorian-era poets who were dually proficient in lyrical and narrative verse.

But to their finest narratives Robinson and Frost bring a level of concision that might be termed cinematic: the tragic-comical tableau of "Mr. Flood's Party," the brisk scene-setting of vignettes such as "Ben Travato" and "Reuben Bright" (a sonnet), or in the case of Frost the cuts and fades in "Home Burial," "The Code," "'Out, Out—,'" and many more.

In further contrast to their nineteenth-century forebears, Robinson and Frost apply an economy of speech and description to reveal character and action. Particularly in the medium of blank verse, the Americans explored the idiomatic possibilities of the poetic line, involving plain-spoken sentences and the rhythms of everyday speech. Robinson, who adored the narrative poet George Crabbe (1754–1832), went on to write the book-length poems *Lancelot* (1920) and *Tristram* (1927). The latter won the Pulitzer Prize for Poetry. Yet it is for his shorter story-poems and the mid-length narrative "Isaac and Archibald" that Robinson will be remembered.

Frost's own contributions to narrative verse are unparalleled. It is already well known that his ability to exploit the tension between ordinary speech and traditional meters conveyed as decisive an impact on subsequent verse as did any of the more celebrated innovations of literary Modernism. But he was also an expert raconteur. Besides the poems already referenced, some of his story-poems include "The Witch of Coös," "The Fear," "A Hundred Collars," and "The Hill Wife."

For many poets in this anthology, Frost is the chief exemplar. Among the great Modernist poets, only he and Robinson Jeffers extended the narrative tradition well into the first quarter of the twentieth century. Jeffers's best-known narratives, "Tamar" and "Roan Stallion," were published together in 1925. Composed in long lines of free verse, these strange poems work as allegories. They show "horizon" and "ambition" all right—to quote again from Edmund Wilson—but they represented a dead end for poets seeking to popularize storytelling in verse.

Poets were far more likely to emulate Frost in the years to come, while Jeffers's mythlike tales of natural beauty and human violence would remain a road not taken.

Throughout the early and mid-twentieth century, narrative also survived in ballad form. One suspects that greater public access and recourse to the blues and the blues lyric played a part. Auden wrote the grimly amusing "Miss Gee" and "Victor" and the late, devotional "Ballad of Barnaby." Other notable ballads, by some of his American contemporaries, include "Captain Carpenter" (John Crowe Ransom), "The Ballad of Billie Potts" (Robert Penn Warren), and—later in the century—"The Ballad of Birmingham" (Dudley Randall), "The Ballad of Rudolph Reed" (Gwendolyn Brooks), and "The Burglar of Babylon" (Elizabeth Bishop).

If Virginia Woolf saw fit to warn earlier poets about an incipient narcissism, what would she have made of the so-called Confessional mode that would thrive in the 1950s and 1960s? A new type of narrative had become popular, but it was inseparable from the poet's personal history.

Memory and experience are rightly considered the raw materials of fiction—but the stories told by these poems invite the reader to visit a singular wound or trauma, more as a destination than a point of departure. The narrative at the heart of Robert Lowell's *Life Studies* (1959) is a prose memoir: "91 Revere Street." Delmore Schwartz likewise planted the semiautobiographical story "In Dreams Begin Responsibility" in his first, eponymous book of poems.

To appreciate the distance traveled from the premodern period, contrast the elaborate stasis in Lowell's "My Last Afternoon with Uncle Devereux Winslow" to the progression of mood and movement in Robinson's "Isaac and Archibald." In both poems, a small boy comes to terms with the fact of mortality while among old people. Each child—through the lens of the first-person adult narrator—views himself dwelling with the ancients: "I was Agrippina / in the Golden House of Nero" (Lowell) and "Agamemnon was a friend of mine" (Robinson).

There end the similarities. Lowell's baroque description of his surroundings, the hopped-up metaphors that make the scenery come alive, do not advance a storyline. That work is done by a bombshell near the end: "He [Lowell's uncle] was dying of the incurable Hodgkin's disease..." Throughout the entire poem, meanwhile—as we are told repeatedly—the child sits on a stone porch, "mixing black earth and lime."

Two contemporaries of Lowell, American poets slightly junior to him, asserted the narrative as a keynote in their own compositions: Anthony Hecht and James Merrill. Like Lowell, both used heavily autobiographical material in their narratives. "More Light! More Light!" and "The Deodand," two story-poems by Hecht, rank with the most devastating verse of the second half of the twentieth century. Neither poem is autobiographical. But neither seems likely to have been written without Hecht's firsthand experiences of obscene violence and cruelty—as an infantryman during World War II, and as a Jew who helped to liberate the concentration camp in Flossenburg, Germany.

For brio and originality, special points must go a third contemporary: Kenneth Koch, author of the book-length poems *Ko: A Season on Earth* (1959) and *The Duplications* (1977), each in *ottava rima* à la Byron. He also published comic treatises such as *The Art of Love* and *The Art of Poetry*. If succeeding poets had emulated Koch's adventurous sallies on form, plot, and discursive writing, then the story of narrative verse in the twentieth century might have unfolded differently. As it happened, the most influential poet in the New York School, with which Koch is associated, was John Ashbery.

Notwithstanding his rhetorical and rhapsodical gifts, and an irresistible playfulness, Ashbery helped to widen the gulf between contemporary poetry and a readership that once had turned to the art form not only for linguistic sorcery but also for stories about people and events. In many Ashbery poems of considerable length, fictional and nonfictional elements are brought in as a kind of scaffolding for what proves ultimately to be a meditative lyric. Such offerings are little more than decoys while he shifts the ground beneath the reader and exposes chance and contingency, undermining the narrative project. Here's the end of "Worsening Situation," from *Self-Portrait in a Convex Mirror* (1975):

One day a man called while I was out
And left this message: "You got the whole thing wrong
From start to finish, Luckily, there's still time
To correct the situation, but you must act fast.

See me at your earliest convenience. And please
Tell no one of this. Much besides your life depends on it."
I thought nothing of it at the time. Lately
I've been looking at old-fashioned plaids, fingering
Starched white collars, wondering whether there's a way
To get them really white again. My wife
Thinks I'm in Oslo—Oslo, France, that is.

The disjunctions in this passage, and in the overall poem, augur a trend that Blake Morrison and Andrew Motion would characterize in their 1982 anthology, *Contemporary British Poetry*. In the preface to that selection, Morrison and Motion note "an interest in narrative" among certain poets then operating in the United Kingdom. "But one important difference between its adoption today and its use by—say—Wordsworth or Tennyson or Frost is that contemporary poets write their stories with more reference to what the process involves. The fact of fictionalizing is relished as it is performed," they explain.

> Where other poets make the familiar strange again through linguistic and metaphoric play, the young narrative poets perform a similar function by drawing attention to the problem of perception. In poems by [James] Fenton and [Tom] Paulin and [Paul] Muldoon and others, we are often presented with stories that are incomplete, or are denied what might normally be considered essential information. The reader is constantly being made to ask, "Who is speaking?" "What are their circumstances and motives?" and "Can they be believed?" There is, moreover, leisure to ponder these questions at length.

The extended lyric that shifts abruptly into a narrative register, but without fulfilling the reader's expectations from narrative—whether in prose or verse—became a staple of much poetry written in the second half of the twentieth century. It is a trend that persists even today.

This brief survey returns us to the starting point of the present volume and provides its raison d'être. The poets in this anthology are writing in the tradition of Hardy, Robinson, and especially Frost, but many of them have also learned from the great writers of narrative verse from the eighteenth and nineteenth centuries. All owe a debt to the presiding spirit of Geoffrey Chaucer. Their poems circulate as a countercurrent, winding past the obstacles that postmodern and post-postmodern aesthetics have thrown in their way.

Beyond the supremacy of the lyric form, and a spate of autobiographical and disjunctive writing, there are other deterrents to narrative verse today. The recent preoccupations of poets with their own cultural and personal identities, and a fear of being labeled inauthentic when trying to assume the voices of people from other backgrounds, rank high among these factors. Indeed, the relative scarcity of short-form narrative poets born from the 1970s through the 2000s, as covered by this anthology, remains a troubling sign for the art. To be sure, most poets who grew up in those decades are still evolving—and who knows where their imaginations might lead them? It is possible, even to be hoped, that this volume will inspire such poets, and their successors, to take up the challenge.

If they do not, then the cost will be borne not only by readers, but also by the greater public consciousness. Whether oral or written, narrative poetry has had a formative role in the identity of most countries and cultures. Stories proceed from a pattern-making instinct. They reorder events and perceptions to convey them acutely and profoundly, just as all poems strive to do with sound, imagery, and formal and linguistic elements. It would be refreshing, even many years from now, to open a poetry manual and see sections about character, plot, setting, and dialogue alongside standard entries on verbal music, lineation, stanza shapes, and other conspicuous aspects of verse. More than any treatise, the following poems justify this vision.

Sunil Iyengar
February 2025

THE COLOSSEUM BOOK OF CONTEMPORARY NARRATIVE VERSE

Jared Carter (b. 1939)

Among authors that Jared Carter has professed to admire are American novelists from the late nineteenth and early twentieth centuries, writers known for their bountiful evocations of regional life. These storytellers include masters of realism such as Sarah Orne Jewett, Willa Cather, and Sherwood Anderson. But Carter has also cited the influence of William Faulkner, who famously found his subject matter by excavating his "own little postage stamp of native soil." Like Faulkner, Carter presents us with a fictional county. Its name is Mississinewa, and though it functions as a composite of several Midwestern towns and farming communities, the county's origins are suggested by the Mississinewa River, a tributary of the Wabash River in eastern Indiana.

Born in Elwood, Indiana, Carter has spent most of his time in his home state, having settled in Indianapolis after military service and travel abroad. Educated at Yale University and Goddard College, Carter began literary life as a small-town reporter in Indiana before working in textbook publishing. His first book, *Work, for the Night Is Coming* (Macmillan, 1981), won the Walt Whitman Award, and his second, *After the Rain* (Cleveland State University Poetry Center, 1993), won the Poets' Prize. His other collections include *Les Barricades Mystérieuses: Thirty-Two Villanelles* (Cleveland State University Poetry Center, 1999) and *The Land Itself* (Monongahela Books, 2019). In 2014, University of Nebraska Press brought out *Darkened Rooms of Summer: New and Selected Poems*.

In recent years, Carter has extolled the merits of classical Chinese and Japanese poetry, and he has been credited with inventing his own short-verse form, the Alexandroid. Craftsmanship over a more extended terrain is on display in both poems here, culled from *After the Rain*. In the first, "Barn Siding," he uses syllabics to spin a dark tale in 130 unrhymed quatrains.

BARN SIDING

It can fetch a dollar a board foot
with the right customer, but I've seen
all the old barns I'm going to mess with
for a while. Got no more need for them.

There's no reason for a man my age
taking risks. Time to pay attention
to what's happened in your life, maybe
pass it along to someone younger.

I never got past eighth grade. Never
worked inside, or had to wear a tie,
or sat at a desk. Learned what I know
the hard way. It helps you remember.

When you get in trouble is when you
start to forget. It happened to me,
looking for barnwood. I got greedy,
forgot what I had learned years before:

if you're putting up kiln-dried lumber
and something starts to crack or splinter,
you've got time to get out of the way;
but old wood won't give any warning.

You take a barn or farmhouse that's stood
a hundred years or more, it's had time
to gravitate, work out all the stress.
The wood's cured; got no more surprises.

Tamper with that balance, and you've got
problems. A house will talk to itself
when the sun hits it, or a cold wind;
it tries to adjust. You've got to hear.

That's what you need in this business: ears.
A picker's always going in places
where he shouldn't be. Has to listen,
know when something's about to happen.

What does a picker do? Picks over
what other people have left behind.
Attics. Basements. Sheds. Like this old place
I knew about in Prophet Township.

There was a woods around it. The bridge
a mile up the road had been out
for years. Nobody came along there
anymore. I kept an eye on it

for a long time. I let others have
first choice. Couples from town like to park
along country lanes. Boys with rifles
come shoot out all the windows. Hoboes,

people who start fires. Old house burns
in a place that far out, no one comes.
Maybe you look across the fields some night,
see a red glow way off in the sky.

I heard the barn didn't burn. Gave it
a few more years, let the new trees get
a toehold. Let the grapevines grow thick.
Then one day I drove out there to see.

What you're looking for is siding with
no color, it's just gone natural
from all that weather. Sometimes the nails
have rusted clear through. You can pry off

big long, smooth pieces with your bare hands.
It's dry, and limber, like old leather
that's been cured right. Every board has what
interior decorators call

"character." If you had gotten up
before daylight and gone out to milk
half a dozen cows, day in, day out
for thirty-odd years, you might call it

something else. But it doesn't matter.
Most of that wood turns out to be pine,
it's full of knots and scattered nail holes,
places where rust has darkened the grain.

I'd been out there all day by myself,
tromping a path through the grass and weeds,
had half a load of tongue-and-groove boards
stacked in the pick-up. Stopped now and then

to try the raspberries growing wild
right up to the double doors. No one
living on that place for thirty years,
limestone chimney where the house had been.

I kept on working. Late afternoon
I took a pair of gloves and a pry-bar
and climbed all the way up to the loft.
Half the floorboards weren't even nailed down.

I fixed up a place to slide them out
a window, took it slow, dropped one plank
at a time down onto the horseweeds.
I'd been up there maybe half an hour,

thought I saw something move. Didn't hear
a thing, just noticed this shadow drift
across the north wall. Sometimes you freeze
before you've had time to think: maybe

it's a mud-dauber hanging there near
your face. Other times your body knows,
takes over, goes where it wants to go,
always brings you out the quickest way.

Even so, I've wondered why that barn
made no noise at all: queen posts starting
to fold in on themselves, rafters, joists,
all those cedar shakes, tons of dry wood

held together for a hundred years,
all beginning to boil, like a storm
brewing, but no thunder, no more sound
than wind making circles in the grass.

I like to think there was nothing left
that could speak, except the wood itself,
everything else was already gone—
grain bin empty, all the old harness

stolen, someone had even climbed up
on the roof to get the lightning rods.
That kind of rod held a big glass ball
people used to say would turn sky blue

from all the current running through it.
You've walked through old houses, or places
that have burnt: nothing but broken cups,
bits of glass, corncobs, heaps of ashes.

Makes you wonder why people would up
and leave a place like that. What happened,
why nobody can make the land pay,
why it all comes up in second growth.

All you hear are stories. This family
tried and lost, that man wore himself out,
this man went out to the barn during
the sale, put a shotgun in his mouth.

You never know why. And there's never
anyone left to tell by the time
some picker stops by to have a look;
there's usually nothing left at all.

There was nothing on this place except
the barn, and nothing left in the barn
except the wood. It had been there all
that time, waiting for the right moment.

Something was holding it together,
some old balance, but when I got down
and pried up that last board, and pushed it
over the edge, the balance was gone

and the whole building simply started
turning itself inside out. The barn
was spiked, and here and there the rain had
gotten in, and turned those hand-made nails

to rust. They lost their grip. Everything
started to slip, unravel, come loose
while I was standing there, and I might
be there still, if it hadn't been for

some part of me that was already
heading toward the ladder and the flight
of stairs down to the ground. Everything
got brighter as I ran, all the cracks

between the siding started to glow
and swell with light. Not a trace of wind,
no tornado screaming through the trees,
sucking on the walls, only layers

of dust and chaff that had built up all
those years working free now and spilling
through the light, leaking, spreading like smoke,
making no more sound than a whisper.

I came down the stairs through dust so thick
I couldn't see. I had almost reached
the barn door when a stray board caught me
across the neck—same place I broke it

twenty years ago, up at the lake—
and drove me straight on through the briars.
That was all that saved me: whatever
breaks is always stronger where it mends.

I don't know how long I was out. When
I came to, it was near dark, and still.
I couldn't move. Paralyzed. The barn
was down. There was nothing I could do,

nobody else knew I was out there.
It might be days, maybe even weeks,
before anybody came that far
and noticed the truck parked in the weeds.

I listened and tried to think. No birds,
that's all I could remember. Pigeons,
sparrows, nothing like that in the loft
when I first went up there. Animals

have a way of knowing. They say cows
will lie down before an earthquake hits.
I listened now. There was a cricket
somewhere in the middle of the barn,

or what used to be the barn, and now
was only a mass of lumber and scrap
no higher than a man. A cricket
first, and then a katydid, somewhere

out in the middle of all that wood.
There were lightning bugs, too, I saw them
winking on and off all around me,
but I couldn't move from where I fell.

I thought I would die then, and be like
everything else, even like the barn,
sinking back into the earth. I felt
peaceful; I could hear all the peepers

and tree frogs and night creatures singing
the way they do every summer night.
They made a sound I had always known
and not thought much about. Now I heard.

They were going to take the barn back,
everything that lived out in that woods—
'possums and squirrels and snakes and bugs.
Now that I thought about it, they were

pickers too, just like me. They came out
when no one else was around, and picked
through whatever happened to be there.
They'd take me too. It wouldn't be long.

When it got dark I could look up through
the raspberry canes and maple leaves
at the stars. They say a man's whole life
runs before him when it's time to die.

I remembered my mother coming
to get me out of bed once, waking
me up so we could go out and see
the northern lights. It was a rare sight

that far south. She held me up, pointing
into the sky. I heard her talking
to my father. They were still young then,
there was something in their voices. What

the northern lights looked like I couldn't
remember. All I could see were stars.
I liked her holding me, and him near.
I looked up at the stars now, lying

on my back, without moving, staring
straight up. They were all still there. The more
I looked the more I could see it's not
really up, at all, but out. We look

out and into. We see from a place
that floats through all that, like a lantern
carried in the dark. I knew no one
would come and find me, but I thought how

you lift the globe, and put in a match,
and the light gives off smoke, until you
turn down the wick, and adjust the flame.
Lower the globe; and now you're all set

to go out and find whatever's lost.
Starting to fall asleep in the dark
I thought I saw something glimmering
like a wick catching fire, like the light

in the barn when it started to shake.
It was daylight, morning. My father
and I were climbing up the steep roof
on our own barn to free a kite stuck

on the weathervane. We threw it down
and then went on to the end. I saw
the lightning rod up close, got to touch
the iron, all scarred and encrusted,

then bent over to look through the ball
of glass the grounding cable ran through.
For a moment I saw everything
through the blue of that ball—down below

the pasture, the creek winding through it,
the four milk cows wading in the smoke
of the willows, the sky reflecting
on the water, the water and grass

and clouds all blue, the whole world blue
as though it had always been that way
and I had never known till I got
to see it through the lightning rod's eye.

I saw it again, lying there, not
able to move—that same blue world,
full of stars now. It was the last thing
I saw before sinking into sleep.

When I woke the next day, I was still
a child, this time looking up at
my own face in a mirror: it moved,
smiled, gazed back at me. Disappeared,

so I could see trees and sky again.
Saw part of her shoulder, then her face
moving around above me, circling,
doing a little dance, looking down

but saying nothing. I tried to speak
but my lips were frozen, no words came.
Help, help, I said in my mind, go get
help, but she was farther away now

and then everything was still. Child.
Little girl. What was she doing here?
Was there anyone with her? and soon
I heard the old woman's voice coming

closer: she was picking her way through
the canes, grumbling when they stuck to her,
sometimes setting the tin buckets down
to get free, warning the child against

spilling berries they'd already picked.
Then it was her face, looking in mine
to see if I was dead or alive,
and seeing something worse than a ghost,

something that had mattered even more
to her than living or dying, once,
a long time ago—me, my own face
but thirty years later now, grown old,

gone sunken and pale, like a wax face
in a coffin. I could see her eyes
while she looked down at me, studying
what to do, even what to say now.

I'd not seen her since that first evening
I got back, in '54, after
two years in Korea. Her folks had
lived out on this place; her dad farmed it.

She and I rode the same school bus;
on rainy days we played in the barn.
And when I joined the Army, she said
she would wait for me, she wrote letters

all that time, and said she was saving
herself for me, that we could get married,
but my younger brother wrote and said
she was going out with other guys.

My first night home we went out to park
in my brother's car. I took off all
her clothes and said now since you've saved it
for me I want it the way the whores

do it in Japan and she started
to cry while I took her on her knees
and made her cry even more and then
pushed her out the door and drove off

with all her clothes. I never knew how
she got home, never saw her again
after I got my discharge papers.
I heard they moved to another state.

And now here she was, it was her, make
no mistake, even with all the lines
and creases and crow's-feet—I could tell.
I could hear her breath coming hard while

she looked down at me, trying to think
what to do next, not even certain
I was still alive. I couldn't blink
or move my eyes. I think she touched me,

touched my face, my body, then my wrist,
feeling for a pulse. I'm still alive,
I tried to say, get me out of here,
I didn't mean it, I'm sorry, I'll

make it up to you somehow, after
all these years. Now she was looking straight
at me. She reached out to touch my face.
"Tears," she said, speaking for the first time.

"Tears. You bastard. Thirty years later
and you're crying." She moved back, out of
my range of vision. I heard her talk
to the little girl, who must have been

a mute. She stood over me again.
Evidently I was still crying—
tears of happiness that she would go,
come back with help, bring an ambulance,

medics, rescue team. "We're going now,"
she said simply. "It won't do to keep
fresh raspberries out in warm weather."
They moved off through the weeds, carrying

both buckets, going slow, bending back
the canes. Everything got calm again.
It was still early morning. I knew
for certain I was going to die now,

and it seemed all right this time, not much
I could do about it anyway.
I started drifting, having dreams with
nothing in them. Whether I woke up

staring into the sky, or whether
I slept till nightfall, I never knew.
Sometime in the night I entered shock;
I was unconscious the next morning.

I had no life signs when they found me
that afternoon, after I had been
lying there for almost two whole days.
Medics came in a helicopter

to lift me out of there, take me down
to a big hospital in the city.
They told me all this later, after
I spent a week in intensive care.

There's always a moment, when you first
wake up in a white room, with nurses
wearing white dresses and little hats,
you think you've died and gone to heaven;

I wasn't dead yet, but I came close.
The man who found me came to see me
in my hospital room. He worked for
the State Police, an interpreter

of aerial photographs. They had
been studying satellite photos
of that part of the world, trying
to see where the Interstate Strangler

might have buried more of his victims.
He picked up young hitchhikers, maybe
offered them money for kinky sex,
took them to abandoned farms not far

off the Interstate. They were handcuffed,
then strangled and mutilated, left
in shallow graves and covered with brush.
They had found seven graves at four sites

and they were looking for more. Sometimes
a fresh grave shows up on a photo
taken by a satellite. Sometimes
they spot a suspicious vehicle

in an unlikely place, or make out
tracks worth investigating. This man
had an old photo that showed the barn
and a brand-new one that showed the barn

changed, in some way, and my pickup parked
at the end of an untraveled lane,
on a farm they already knew was
abandoned, on their list to watch close.

They sent a team out right away with
guns drawn in case it was the Strangler
holed up there, and of course they found me
in his place. My paralysis was

only temporary. I walked out
of that hospital a week later,
a bit stiff but still able to climb
in my truck—the troopers brought it there—

and drive home. They had confiscated
the half load of barn siding but dropped
the trespassing charge. The county paid
the medevac for rescuing me,

the state picked up the tab for my stay
in the hospital. I don't know why—
maybe they added it to the cost
of catching the Strangler. They got him

a month later—by that time they knew
he drove a pickup, and this was in
all the newspapers and on TV.
A driver on the Interstate saw

a hitchhiker get in a pickup
and memorized the license number
and phoned it in to the State Police
from the next rest stop. The Strangler

gave up after a high-speed chase through
three counties. They say he'll get the chair.
Me, I gave up picking barn siding.
I work strictly on old houses now,

sometimes garages. There's a demand
for copper; the price is going up.
I can rip it out of those old walls,
those basements, better than anyone.

I have to listen, pay attention,
like always. I don't want those shadows
sneaking up on me again. Sometimes
I think I died out there in the weeds

next to where that barn fell in, and I'm
a different person now, born again
but in a strange way. Sometimes I think
it was God who looked down through the lens

of that satellite camera and
saw me lying there. Sometimes I think
it was me who looked out through the eye
of the lightning rod, and saw something

that might have been God. And then there was
Retta showing up like that, as though
no time had passed, and how I asked her
to forgive me, even though I knew

she couldn't hear me. For a while
I thought she had left me there to die.
Then I understood it could have been
a lot worse. She might have had a knife

or a pair of pruning shears. No one
would have known. When they found my body,
the coroner would have chalked it up
to the Strangler. She didn't do that,

she simply went away with the girl
and the berries. It's odd to think how
even the Strangler could have passed through
a place like that, looking for something

and not finding it, then moving on.
Nobody's lived on that old farm since
the early nineteen-fifties, nothing's
left there now but a bunch of trees set

back from the road. The other pickers
will have cleaned up the barnwood by now,
carried it off like a swarm of ants
at a picnic. One of these years when

the freeze and thaw works enough mortar
from between the stones, and the chimney
blows over, there won't be anything
left there except the raspberry patch.

People will still stop by—different
kinds of pickers, the ones who know where
the hickory nuts fall, out in the woods,
and where to find the best shaggymanes

and puffballs, and when it's time to look
for morels. Those people are shadows
moving along the edges, always
keeping a step ahead. Finding things

can be a calling, a way of life.
All a picker wants to do is find
something nobody else knows about,
have it for a while, then pass it on.

This story I've been telling you now,
you might say you just ran across it
by accident, but the plain truth is
we don't hear things until we're ready

and that could be a kind of finding,
too, even a way of life—paying
attention to what's happening now,
then handing it on to someone else.

You take those young men the Strangler found
standing at the side of the highway,
or waiting in one of those rest stops,
hoping for a ride to the next town:

they're no different from the rest of us,
they've come to see there's no going back,
everything is gone now, or changed from
the way it used to be. There's no shame

in what they did. They say he would talk
about helping them out, would tell them
that just past this next exit he knew
of a man who needed a good hand

to work for him for a day or two,
in this old farmhouse, fixing it up,
getting it ready to sell again.
If you hadn't eaten anything

for two or three days, or hadn't slept,
if you were flat broke and couldn't seem
to get a ride, you'd listen to him,
you'd want him to like you, be willing

to go with him while he keeps turning
down those deserted roads, those old lanes
where the signs are full of bullet holes
and the apple trees have all gone wild.

Then think of the satellite out there
in space mapping that part of the world,
looking down and seeing everything,
catching it just before it changes

but not knowing what anything is—
maybe seeing Retta and the child
walking along with their tin buckets,
maybe seeing me sliding old boards

down out of that barn loft, the Strangler
parked in the truck, talking to the boy—
while this shadow drifts out over us,
the one we can never really know.

THE PURPOSE OF POETRY

This old man grazed thirty head of cattle
in a valley just north of the covered bridge
on the Mississinewa, where the reservoir
stands today. Had a black border collie
and a half-breed sheep dog with one eye.
The dogs took the cows to pasture each morning
and brought them home again at night
and herded them into the barn. The old man
would slip a wooden bar across both doors.
One dog slept on the front porch, one on the back.

He was waiting there one evening
listening to the animals coming home
when a man from the courthouse stopped
to tell him how the new reservoir
was going to flood all his property.
They both knew he was too far up in years
to farm anywhere else. He had a daughter
who lived in Florida, in a trailer park.
He should sell now and go stay with her.
The man helped bar the doors before he left.

He had only known dirt under his fingernails
and trips to town on Saturday mornings
since he was a boy. Always he had been around
cattle, and trees, and land near the river.
Evenings by the barn he could hear the dogs
talking to each other as they brought in
the herd; and the cows answering them.
It was the clearest thing he knew. That night
he shot both dogs and then himself.
The purpose of poetry is to tell us about life.

Bob Dylan (b. 1941)

In the finest of Bob Dylan's songs from the 1960s and early to mid-1970s, the words roused a fervor of admiration denied to the best lyric poets of the era. Many of those pieces use narrative devices such as dialogue and shifting points of view. Less prevalent is sustained storytelling; among exceptions are "The Lonesome Ballad of Hattie Carroll" (*The Times They Are A-Changin'*, 1964), "The Ballad of Frankie Lee and Judas Priest" (*John Wesley Harding*, 1967), and "Isis" (*Desire*, 1976). Although it is customary to attach Dylan, especially in his early work, to the bardic traditions of American folk and blues singers, he has also acknowledged a debt to the Beat poets and, in his acceptance speech for the 2016 Nobel Prize in Literature, to *Moby Dick*. Several songs on his 1970 album *New Morning* sprang from an ill-fated collaboration with the poet Archibald MacLeish.

Beyond song lyrics, literary contributions by this Hibbing, Minnesota, native—born Robert Zimmerman—include *Tarantula* (Scribner, 1971), *Chronicles: Volume One* (Simon & Schuster, 2004), and *The Philosophy of Modern Song* (Simon & Schuster, 2022). "Seven Curses" is adapted from an English folk ballad that has been passed down with various titles; versions were recorded by Lead Belly (1888–1949) and John Jacob Niles (1892–1980), two of Dylan's early influences. His own recording of the song, from 1961, surfaced on *The Bootleg Series, Vol. 1–3: Rare & Unreleased 1961–1991* (1991). The second entry is taken from *Blood on the Tracks* (1975), though verse 12 of the published lyric is not heard on the album version.

SEVEN CURSES

Old Reilly stole a stallion
But they caught him and they brought him back
And they laid him down on the jailhouse ground
With an iron chain around his neck

Old Reilly's daughter got a message
That her father was goin' to hang
She rode by night and came by morning
With gold and silver in her hand

When the judge he saw Reilly's daughter
His old eyes deepened in his head
Sayin', "Gold will never free your father
The price, my dear, is you instead"

"Oh I'm as good as dead," cried Reilly
"It's only you that he does crave
And my skin will surely crawl if he touches you at all
Get on your horse and ride away"

"Oh father you will surely die
If I don't take the chance to try
And pay the price and not take your advice
For that reason I will have to stay"

The gallows shadows shook the evening
In the night a hound dog bayed
In the night the grounds were groanin'
In the night the price was paid

The next mornin' she had awoken
To know that the judge had never spoken
She saw that hangin' branch a-bendin'
She saw her father's body broken

These be seven curses on a judge so cruel:
That one doctor will not save him
That two healers will not heal him
That three eyes will not see him

That four ears will not hear him
That five walls will not hide him
That six diggers will not bury him
And that seven deaths shall never kill him

LILY, ROSEMARY AND THE JACK OF HEARTS

The festival was over, the boys were all plannin' for a fall
The cabaret was quiet except for the drillin' in the wall
The curfew had been lifted and the gamblin' wheel shut down
Anyone with any sense had already left town
He was standin' in the doorway lookin' like the Jack of Hearts

He moved across the mirrored room, "Set it up for everyone," he said
Then everyone commenced to do what they were doin' before he
  turned their heads
Then he walked up to a stranger and he asked him with a grin
"Could you kindly tell me, friend, what time the show begins?"
Then he moved into the corner, face down like the Jack of Hearts

Backstage the girls were playin' five-card stud by the stairs
Lily had two queens, she was hopin' for a third to match her pair
Outside the streets were fillin' up, the window was open wide
A gentle breeze was blowin', you could feel it from inside
Lily called another bet and drew up the Jack of Hearts

Big Jim was no one's fool, he owned the town's only diamond mine
He made his usual entrance lookin' so dandy and so fine
With his bodyguards and silver cane and every hair in place
He took whatever he wanted to and he laid it all to waste
But his bodyguards and silver cane were no match for the Jack of Hearts

Rosemary combed her hair and took a carriage into town
She slipped in through the side door lookin' like a queen without
  a crown
She fluttered her false eyelashes and whispered in his ear
"Sorry, darlin', that I'm late," but he didn't seem to hear
He was starin' into space over at the Jack of Hearts

"I know I've seen that face before," Big Jim was thinkin' to himself
"Maybe down in Mexico or a picture up on somebody's shelf"
But then the crowd began to stamp their feet and the houselights
did dim
And in the darkness of the room there was only Jim and him
Starin' at the butterfly who just drew the Jack of Hearts

Lily was a princess, she was fair-skinned and precious as a child
She did whatever she had to do, she had that certain flash every time
she smiled
She'd come away from a broken home, had lots of strange affairs
With men in every walk of life which took her everywhere
But she'd never met anyone quite like the Jack of Hearts

The hangin' judge came in unnoticed and was being wined and dined
The drillin' in the wall kept up but no one seemed to pay it any mind
It was known all around that Lily had Jim's ring
And nothing would ever come between Lily and the king
No, nothin' ever would except maybe the Jack of Hearts

Rosemary started drinkin' hard and seein' her reflection in the knife
She was tired of the attention, tired of playin' the role of
Big Jim's wife
She had done a lot of bad things, even once tried suicide
Was lookin' to do just one good deed before she died
She was gazin' to the future, riding on the Jack of Hearts

Lily washed her face, took her dress off and buried it away
"Has your luck run out?" she laughed at him, "Well, I guess you must
have known it would someday
Be careful not to touch the wall, there's a brand-new coat of paint
I'm glad to see you're still alive, you're lookin' like a saint"
Down the hallway footsteps were comin' for the Jack of Hearts

The backstage manager was pacing all around by his chair
"There's something funny going on," he said, "I can just feel it
in the air"
He went to get the hangin' judge, but the hangin' judge was drunk
As the leading actor hurried by in the costume of a monk
There was no actor anywhere better than the Jack of Hearts

Lily's arms were locked around the man that she dearly loved to touch
She forgot all about the man she couldn't stand who hounded her
so much
"I've missed you so," she said to him, and he felt she was sincere
But just beyond the door he felt jealousy and fear
Just another night in the life of the Jack of Hearts

No one knew the circumstance but they say that it happened
pretty quick
The door to the dressing room burst open and a cold revolver clicked
And Big Jim was standin' there, ya couldn't say surprised
Rosemary right beside him, steady in her eyes
She was with Big Jim but she was leanin' to the Jack of Hearts

Two doors down the boys finally made it through the wall
And cleaned out the bank safe, it's said that they got off with
quite a haul
In the darkness by the riverbed they waited on the ground
For one more member who had business back in town
But they couldn't go no further without the Jack of Hearts

The next day was hangin' day, the sky was overcast and black
Big Jim lay covered up, killed by a penknife in the back
And Rosemary on the gallows, she didn't even blink
The hangin' judge was sober, he hadn't had a drink
The only person on the scene missin' was the Jack of Hearts

The cabaret was empty now, a sign said, "Closed for repair"
Lily had already taken all of the dye out of her hair
She was thinkin' 'bout her father, who she very rarely saw
Thinkin' 'bout Rosemary and thinkin' about the law
But most of all she was thinkin' 'bout the Jack of Hearts

Charles Martin (b. 1942)

"Passages from Friday," the first entry below, is one of the two best poems that American literature has produced in answer to Daniel Defoe's *Robinson Crusoe* (1719). The other is Elizabeth Bishop's (1911–79) "Crusoe in England." Strictly as narrative, however, and for its innovations in orthography, Martin's offering is superior. Also admirable is how completely the poet enters into the sensibility of the fictional Native American and transfigures it. But for many readers, the most salient aspect will be Martin's adeptness at the rhyming quatrains of which the poem is constituted.

Writing in formal verse traditions, he is a poet-translator of extensive range. *Starting from Sleep: New and Selected Poems* (The Overlook Press, 2002) was chosen by the American Academy of Poets as a finalist for the Lenore Marshall Award. Two years later, the same organization honored him with the Morton Landon Translation Award for his version of Ovid's *Metamorphoses* (W. W. Norton, 2003). As a translator of Latin verse, Martin has also published *The Poems of Catullus* (Johns Hopkins University Press, 1989) and an eponymous study of the poet (Yale University Press, 1992). In 2012, he and Gavin Flood completed *The Bhagavad Gita: A New Translation* (W. W. Norton). A translation of Euripedes's *Medea* (University of California Press) followed in 2019. The same decade saw two original volumes from Martin: *Signs & Wonders* (2011) and *Future Perfect* (2018). Both are published by Johns Hopkins University Press, which in 2025 brought out a new collection, *The Khayyam Suite*.

In the course of his career, Martin has won an award in literature from the American Academy of Arts and Letters, fellowships from the National Endowment for the Arts and the Ingram Merrill Foundation, a Pushcart Prize, and the Poetry Foundation's Bess Hokin Prize. Born in New York City, he graduated from Fordham University and earned an MA and a PhD from the State University of New York in Buffalo. Martin has taught at Johns Hopkins University, Queensborough Community College, Syracuse University, City University of New York, the Sewanee Writers' Conference, and the West Chester Poetry Conference, among many other places.

"Passages from Friday" originally appeared in 1983 in a limited edition of 250 copies (Abattoir Editions, University of Oklahoma Press).

PASSAGES FROM FRIDAY

In a little Time, I began to speak
to him, and teach him to speak to me;
having sav'd him on the 6th Day of the Week,
I made him know that his Name was to be

Friday; *I thought it right to call him so*
for the Memory of the Time; in the same Way
I taught him to say Master; then let him know
from this Day on, that was to be my Name.

I

With my owne thoro' un-Worthyness
of Ways befor my Face I turn to
this burthensom Task which nevertheless
being decided, *Viz.* That I must learn to

write as my *Master* did & so set down
tho' withowt any Hope of Recovery
from this inchanted Island to my owne
Nation whence taken in Captivity

som Yeers a go: That by the diligent
copying of Letters from his Bokes
now my owne I ha' further'd this Intent
to sutch Degree wher all most now it looks

if I may say so now it makes me think
that Heaven smiles upon my Enterprise:
That having got a Quantity of Ink
at no great Cost express'd from native Berries

sutch as may express my Native Wit
most suitably, if I may so conceive:
That having obtain'd sutch Fethers as are fit
to write with, once sharpen'd, I will now leave

all mis-givings as to my Ability
& here invoke all-mighty *Providence:*
That having from my *Master* a Supply
of What to write on, I will now commence

with an Accownt of my Deliverance
as this commenc'd my *new* or 2nd Life;
for, being ignorant of *Providence*
& its Design, I cling'd to the Belief

that thos seiz'd in War-fare cou'd be eaten;
this, I had learn'd, was what my *God* intended:
So, when my owne Nation was defeated
& I took Prisoner, it seem'd my Life was ended;

truss'd up & cast into a War-Canoo
I lay as one all ready Dead & thought
ownly of, *What my Enemy wou'd do*.
Soon at this Island I was abruptly brought

to Sacrifice, as one by 1 my 3
Fellowes were knock'd down, cut open & burn'd:
One still a live, twisting so in Agony
that it a mews'd my Captor, the Fellow turn'd

to watch the Sport: Up I leap & race
as swiftly as I can a long the Shoar:
A Cry goes up: Two of my Foes give Chace:
I run from them till I can run no more

when suddenly a Cross my Path ther flies
what seems a Mountain, cover'd all in Hair!
I tumble Grownd-ward, a trembling with Surprise:
Have I escap'd the Snell but for the Snare?

This *Mountain* proves *Volcano*, belching Fire
that strikes the foremost of my Persuers Dead
at which the 2nd one runs off in Terror;
I place the *Masters* Foot upon my Head.

II
My Beginning begun, I must begin agayn
for, tho' my *Master* is no longer a live,
his Spirit guides the Movement of my Pen
a Cross this Sheet, commanding me: *To give*

a true Account of owr Life together
in all Particulars: How each Day was spent
from 1st Light, when I go off to gather
Fewel for the Fire lay'd owt Side his Tent

then fetch his Cloathes for him & lay them owt:
Then leve him be now: Run off to prepare
his Goats-Flesh Stewe; this done, I hear him showt:
Bring him his Jugg: I fetch it in & pour

him a great Supp to drink, whilst he dresses
& then attend him till his Stewe is eaten
& then if all has not been as he pleases
as like as not poor *Friday* will get beaten;

then off to tend the Flock whos swolne Dams
bleating together urgently complain
of my Neglect; an Howre on my Hams
& thence to gather up what Scraps remain

after my *Master*; next to weed the Corn
which occupies my Time befor his Dinner
must be prepar'd; so passes the Morn;
It is because poor Friday *is a Sinner*

that he must spend his Days Gain-fully toiling,
my Master tells me; I slice his Bread & Chees
& bast with Grees the Joynt of Goat-Flesh broiling;
whil he has Dinner, *Friday* takes his Ease.

The after Noon was spent a frighting Game;
Parrots especially he lov'd to kill,
for, having taught 1 once to say his Name,
that one, escaping, had pass'd on the Skill

to others of the brightly Fether'd Race;
so then, wherever in the Woods we go
from Tree to Tree a Head of us they chace
crying, *Robinson   Robinson   Crusoe*

Heedless of wasted Powder when he's vext
he fires off his Peeces 1 by 1
whil *Parrots* fly from one Tree to the next
crying, *Crusoe   Crusoe   Robinson*

III
I mind 1 Time we bilded us a Raft
which, he say'd was, *A Work of no little Art*;
but the Islands Magick overcame his Craft
& the first Tide that took it, shook it a Part

& left the Peeces scatter'd on the Shoar;
for the Island held him firmly in its Grip
& wou'd not let go. It was not long befor
he had a nother Plan: *We wou'd bild a Ship*

out of a hallow'd Log. Weeks must be spent
in searching of the Mountains for a Tree
that wou'd, in all Things, answer his Intent;
at last we found owr Selves a *Mahagonny*

which, he was sure, wou'd serve his Purpose well.
I guess'd it wou'd not, for when we found it
This Tree commenc'd groaning; when we began to fell
the lesser Trees that grew up all a round it

thes groan'd as well; I hear'd, but the *Master* cou'd not;
earnestly I begg'd him, *To find a nother*
Tree, but he was adamant & wou'd not
hear of sutch Talk; a Cuffing for my Bother.

Now after we had cleer'd a Way the Grownd
came the feeling of this prodigious Tree
no Tree at all, but a Womans Spryght imprison'd
which, as we cut it, moan'd so piteously

that owr Axes were enchanted by
the Sownd to sutch Degree that they lept back
in owr Hands, *as tho' they'd rather try*
owr Flesh than hers. After 1 sutch Attack

I saw that *Master* had been somewhat nick'd
by my owne Blade, which I at once let go;
I seiz'd his wounded Hand in mine & lick'd
the Blood a Way, as any Man wou'd do

owt of meer Affection; he wrenches loos
his Hand from mine & violently throes
me to the Grownd with scurrilous Abuse
& drives me from him with repeated Kicks & Blows.

IV

An Howre every Evening was given
to my Instruction, by which, however
imperfectly, I learn'd of *Hell & Heaven*,
the *Middle Way*, the *Pulley & the Lever*

& many a nother Use-full Invention,
astownding to me, who had mis-understood
so mutch befor; I soon form'd the Intention
of becoming as like my *Master* as I cou'd,

putting the *Cannibal* of earlier Yeers
behind me; and yet, my owne Ignorance
both hinder'd me & rais'd my *Masters* Fears
of my Savage Nature. *This* Callibans

a Canniball, he'd say: *No teaching him.*
Nevertheless, I learn'd how *God* and the *Devill*
must wage continuous War-Fare till the End of Time
or thenabowts, when *God* will putt an End to Evil;

& how to load & fire Fowling-Peeces
& cleen then after-ward; and how to cloathe
my self in Goat-Skins & to make Cheeses
from the Goats-Milk; and so on & so forth;

untill so mutch of what my *Master* knew,
I knew as well, quickly comprehending
even the meaner Things he taught me to do,
(Viz.) *cooking, cleaning-up, sewing & mending*;

and yet, tho' I did all I cou'd to plees,
learning to do & doing all I learn'd,
his Melancholy seem'd ownly to increes,
as tho' in his Innards a low Feaver burn'd.

V

When the Moons Light pours a Cross my Window-Sill
I spread my Writing owt upon my Knees
losing my Self for Howres in it till
my Wick of Oakum sputters in its Grees

& I nodd off. I had fell to dreaming
of once, when I, return'd to the Plantation
with Raizins for his Wine, I hear'd him screaming
as tho' persu'd by the whol *Caribb* Nation;

I rush'd froward, determin'd either to aid
him in his Struggle, or to fall besyde;
no one a peer'd to be at the Stockade
when I paws'd ther breefly for a Look inside;

rather I found him wher the Beasts were penn'd
& they all murther'd. He had slyt ther Throats
& as they twitch'd & skitter'd on the Grownd
he hack'd & slash'd at thes poor harm-less Goats

then order'd me to. *Bild a great big Fire;*
Naught may be sav'd of them at all, he say'd;
Let Flames consume ther Carckasses entire.
Now many of these Beasts were scarsly Dead

& others, all tho' dismember'd still liv'd;
yet in my Fear, I none the less obey'd him,
sutch whippings & picklings as I receiv'd
whenever I objected or gainsay'd him.

Later, he say'd that the Goats had learn'd his Name
by listening to the escap'd *Parrots*
& wou'd repeat it, braying, for a Game
till he was phrenzied. I say it was Spirits

that wait a bowt a Man to do him Harm
when they are able; thes infest the Island.
The Beasts being burn'd, he became quite calm
& for 3 Days remain'd a Loan in Silence.

When he came forth he went to the ruin'd Pen
& cast the Spirits owt in Peels of Laughter,
till at the last, he seem'd him-self agayn;
yet never wou'd he speak a bowt this after.

VI

But I digress here, having yet to tell
of, How we got the Tree down for owr *Canoo*;
after a whil, I offer'd to cast a Spell
to quieten the Womans Spirit, who

dwelt within it; I did a little Dance
& sprinkl'd the Grownd a round the Tree with Grain
mix'd with some Blood; the Spryght fell into Silence
& owr Axe-Blades obey'd us once agayn.

Master pretended not to see this at all
until I had finish'd. We girdl'd it a round
then left it to bleed & dry; after severall
Weeks he came back & brought it to the Grownd.

Painfull Labour follow'd, for we must peel
all of the Bark a Way; then burn & scrape
the In-sides off with glowing Coals untill
it was hallow'd owt; then we must shape

the Out-side Part; and all of the Work we did,
owr endless toiling & incessant Care
serv'd only to show, *the Woman that was hid;*
at last her Figur was brought owt so cleer

that *Master* saw her, as he him-self confess'd;
and none of owr toiling cou'd efface
1 single Curve of Belly, Thigh, or Breast.
I judg'd her to be a Woman of my Race

by Virtue of her Colour, dark as the Grayn
of that *Mahagonee* in which we found her.
Perhaps she too was brought here to be slayn
& had escap'd when her Captors unbound her

for a Moment; and running off as I did,
but finding no *Master*, no Deliverance
from her persuing Enemies, she hid
her-self by taking leave of her Womans

Body & becoming at once a meer Tree;
her Roots sunk down, her Branches lifted high,
she blossom'd into a Security
that lasted until we 2 hapn'd by.

VII

Of thos sever'd Branches I mutch later made
my *European Figur Fetisches*,
7 in Number, painted & array'd
a long the Shoar to ward off Savages

& to attrackt thos Shipps I some Times spy'd
at a great Distance; by they never came neer
all tho' at some Times the Savages did,
when, after War-fare they brought Captives heer

to feast upon them. I some Times discover'd
Remainders of ther Feasts upon the Sand
or in it, when my prodding Toe uncover'd
an eyeless Skull, a blackned Foot or Hand;

ther were 7 of thes Figurs, as I say'd;
and all of them stood facing owt to Sea
with Musket in one Hand & a naked Blade
in the other, scowling ferociously.

Often I try'd, but never succeeded,
in a wakening them; that Enterprise
was doom'd, for What my Europeans needed
was not my dancing, but a Shipps Supplies;

more Hats & Cloathes & shiny buckl'd Shoes,
more Axes, Muskets, Cannon & Gun-Powder,
more of sutch Goods than they cou'd ever use;
ownly such Abundance cou'd have rows'd them.

I danc'd abowt & summon'd them to dance
but they ignor'd my importunate Commotion;
fix'd in ther Places as tho' in a Trance,
staring with painted Eyes at the great Ocean.

VIII

My *Masters* plan was this: Ther was a Stream
1 hundred Yards or so up-Hill of owr
Camp; in the rainy Season, it became
a raging Torrent, into which we'd lower

over *Peragua*, as he lik'd to call it;
and let that Torrent bring it down to Sea.
I ask'd him, *How we wou'd ever haul it*
thos hundred Yards? He answer'd, *I wou'd be*

a Beast of Burthen, which do not complayn
no Matter how heavy the Tasks theyr made to do;
he wou'd be likewise, for, *Who grutches Pain*
that have at last Deliverance in View?

And so we begun. Despite his good Intent
the Labour was inequally divided:
Whenever Shoulders were needed, *Fridays* bent;
whenever Decisions, *Master* decided.

Rollers were cut & lay'd a long the Grownd
a Part of the Way, and the *Canoo* was hoist
upon them: Ropes from her bow were run a round
a Windlass, which my *Master* had devis'd;

and when we turn'd this Windless, owr *Canoo*
seem'd to a waken; it shudder'd & groan'd
& slid upon thes Rollers for a few
Yards at a time, till owr Rope was wound

a round the Windlass; or the Rope broke through;
or the Wind-less broke down; or a Roller slid
owt of the Way & stranded the Canoo;
or, if som other Thing cou'd fail, it did;

for nothing he ever did was done with Ease
of Natur; for, according to *Providence*,
all Things had Value ownly from ther Use,
& had no *Feelings* nor *Intelligence*,

which we call *Spirit*; and which they did withowt;
he call'd me *Savage*, that I cou'd not see
how Things were Tools & how thes Tools allow'd
us to master mor Things: For it appear'd to me

that it was them that master'd us; by making
us work so mutch for What we little needed;
and, when we wanted them, by all Ways breaking;
so that they labour'd rather less than we did.

IX

1 took 2 Months befor we reach'd the Stream,
but we were not yet done; *Master* intended,
That the *Canoo* must be slung owt in between
2 opposing Trees, hoist up & suspended

over the Creek, that, once the Flood began
she cou'd be launch'd withowt being swept a Way;
had all Things hapned according to his Plan—
but that they did not, I scarsly need say.

We got the Boat slung in betwixt the Trees
& hoist her up; and then went back to move
owr Camp to the Creek; and then took owr Ease,
he in a Tent & I in the *Canoo*,

which, like a Hammock, lull'd me into Slumber;
I saw my Self (cradl'd in my Dream
by yeelding Flesh, not by unyeelding Timber)
sleeping once mor in my owne Mothers Womb,

as in the Waters under-neath the Earth;
I felt her Body shuddering & trembling
& knew that soon I wou'd be dropp'd in Birth;
and in my Ears hear'd a thund'rous rumbling

which suddenly stopp'd: Now I hear'd someone call
my Name, and sitting up, saw my *Master* drench'd
upon the Bank, poynting to the Wattery Wall
that, at the next Moment, crash'd on me & launch'd

owr *Canoo* onto the swolne River
with me In-side it; tho' not, I fear'd, for long;
as the *Canoo*, a Log once more, roll'd over
& whipp'd a bowt, was taken up & flung

now heer, now ther, now up & now below,
compell'd to dance the Rivers merry Dance;
I griev'd for my *Master*, losing at one Blow
his ownly Servant & his Deliverance,

& shed more Tears for him, than for my Self.
What hapned after this was Wonder-full:
As in my Dream, Wood melted into Flesh
& a warm Hand press'd me to the Hull

a Hull no longer: For the Flood releas'd
the Woman that was hid in the *Canoo*
& with me clinging tightly to her Waist
she swum & frollick'd like a *Whale* or *Sea-Cow*;

I was no longer afraid now of Death,
tho' we dove down Water-Falls immensely high
into the deep Pools that had form'd beneath,
then let the Current take us by & by

the 2 of us at one with the Water
& she cavorting in it merrily
& the arch'd Trees echoing with her Laughter:
As *Dolphins* carry Children, she carry'd me,

my Arms & Legs secure a bowt her fastned:
When she roll'd over on her Belly, I twin'd her
Hair in my Hands
great Coils of black Hair glisten'd
like *Water-Serpents* streaming owt behind her

X

When *Master* found me at the Streams Embouchure
his Joy in finding that I had not dy'd
seem'd nicely balanc'd by his Discomfiture;
at first kissing & embraceing me, he cry'd

Thou art a live why then I'm not a Loan;
but then his Smiles were driven off by Tears:
O wher has the Hope of my Deliverance gone?
He thwack'd and pummel'd me a bowt the Ears

until his Arms, exhausted by this Game,
sank to his Sides and he sunk down be Side
me on the Sand wher I'd sank down the same
& then embrac'd me once more & once more cry'd

but beat on me no more. We stay'd like that
for quite a whil, and then he ask'd, *What hapned*
to his Canoo? *Was it stove in or what?*
I told him all that I ha' just now written

except for, What he had all ready seen,
viz, how it broak a Way; but I told him how
it chang'd into the Woman who had been
trapp'd in the Tree, *et cetera*; and how

she carry'd me, once she had gotten owt,
down the whol River, till we came at length
to where he found me, by the Rivers Mouth;
to all of which he listen'd to in Silence,

nodding his Head ownly, a little Bit;
so I went on further, telling him of my
Distress, when I gather'd that she meant to quit
the Island all together, seeing that I

must choose betwicks my *Freedom* & my *Master*,
to whom I ow'd so mutch; here, *Master* nodded:
Lengthening her Stroaks, she swum mutch faster,
heading Sea-ward; till I cry'd owt & prodded

her Flanks with my Toes to-wards the Island;
then she roll'd over on her Back & pick'd me up
& look'd at me for a great long Whil and
smil'd at me, *as at a poor, bedraggl'd Pup,*

for sutch I must ha' seem'd to her no Doubt;
then dropp'd me in be-Side her, and with the
Palm of her Hand, gave me a Push; I struck owt
for the Island, and in a little Whil I'd swum

back to the Rivers Mowth; once safely a Shoar
I try'd to spot her, but she had disappear'd,
and I never saw that Woman any more,
and so I lay down, being suddenly tir'd.

Master say'd nothing, when I was all done,
but meerly sat with his Chin upon his Breast
staring with Eyes vacant of Expression:
When I ask'd him, *If he did not wish to rest,*

he rose & totter'd off on down the Beach;
when he return'd, he had in Hand a few
Peeces of Wood which he had found & which
he say'd was from the broaken-up *Canoo*;

Not possible, says I; but he ignor'd
my owne Account, as, *It did not make Sense*:
Why, no sutch Thing as that never occur'd,
Or wou'd I mock both him & Providence?

XI

At first I little thought how hard my *Master*
took the Loss of owr *Peragua-Canoo*;
but it prov'd, as he say'd, *1 Disaster*
too many for him: That, having gone thro'

sutch a vast Labour of ungrutching Pain
& when Deliverance was near on Hand
to have his bright Hopes extinguish'd by the Rain:
Why, this was too mutch for any Man to stand,

He'd say, shaking his Head in Dis-belief.
And after this, he grew Absent in his Mind,
talking to him-self, mainly, and wandering off
into the Woods with his Jugg of Raisin Wine.

One Evening an Accident occur'd
which left hin neer Dead, tho' not entirely:
whil I was cleaning up, he disappear'd,
taking a long his Jugg for Company;

he must ha' wander'd for a good long Time,
pawsing every now & agayn for a Swig;
soon good & lost, he must ha' try'd to climb
a Hill to get his Bearings; but he & the Jugg,

with him half-fill'd & it half-empty, spill'd
down a steep Sloap until a scrubby Oak
shatter'd the one & very nearly kill'd
the other; inducing in him sutch a Stroak

as left him helpless. When I reach'd him, he
lay withowt moving & ownly roll'd his Eyes
a round his Head as tho' beseeching me
for some Thing or other; but other Wise

he was incapable of Movement or Speech;
I did What little I cou'd do for him
ther & then carry'd him down to the Beach,
& then, the next Day, by easy Stages Home.

Despite my Care for him, he did not regayn
any of thos Powers lost in his Fall;
since Death was certain, I told him of my Plan;
viz., That incertain of *Christian* Buriall,

not having yet been taught by him in this,
but at the same Time, being a *Heathen* no more,
I had som Notions of the Sacrifice
& Ceremony proper to insure

his Souls Release. I thought it for the best
not to belabour this; but meerly to repeat
the Words of his Saviour at the last Feast,
when to his Fellowes, he say'd, *Take ye & eat*

of my owne Flesh in the Remembrance of me;
he seem'd mutch agitated as I spoak
& very pleas'd, as ownly I cou'd see;
but of course, he cou'd say nothing for his Stroak.

XII
Draw a sharp Blade a round the Neck of the Goat
& all 4 Hooves, then make a nother Slyt
with your Knife right at the Base of the Throat
over the Wind-Pipe & then lengthen it,

drawing the Knife down-wards from that Poynt
in a firm Manner, moving down the Breast
& going on until you come to the Vent;
the Knife Blade shou'd not be too firmly press'd

or the Bagg will rupture, souring the Flesh;
remove the In-sides & scrub owt the Cavity
with Handfulls of twisted Grasses to keep in fresh;
& now the Skin will come off easily,

in 1 single Peece, once the Lymms ha' been slyt
exactly as was mention'd up above;
then work your Blade in betwixt Flesh & Pelt
& peel the latter back-wards like a Glove;

be carefull not to press with the Blade too hard
or you will tear the Pelt; when it's remov'd
use a sharpen'd Shell to scrape a way the Lard
& Gristle clinging to the In-side; then shave

the Hairs clean off the Out-side; pound to soften
& then stretch it owt to dry in the Sun;
after some Time it will most likely stiffen;
then take it down & pound it once agayn,

softlier this Time; after somemore of this
you will find owt, that in a little While
the Skin of your Goat will mutch resemble his
& may be us'd as Parchment for your Quill.

XIII

Now being my Self entirely a Loan
upon the Island & somewhat at a Loss
for what to do, having so long done
as I was bidden, I waited for his Voice;

and whil I was waiting, I begun to bild
my *Figur Fetisches* a long the Shoar;
and finding that this Occupation fill'd
my Days agreeably, I bilded some more:

When no Ships came, I made up for the Lack
by bilding 1 of Drift-wood Scraps & Peeces;
and, as my Shipps wanted Heathens to attack,
I went to wher the Cannibals had feasted;

tho' not withowt considerable Anxiety;
and after picking Care-fully thro' the Sand
I made some whol *Cannibals* from a Variety
of Parts; taking them from this 1 heer a Hand

and from that 1 over ther a broakin Skull
or something els which he no longer needed,
& set them owt to menace my Drift-wood Hull
on Wooden Sticks; after this I added

more Europeans to flesh owt my Crew,
carv'd owt of Wood, with Rifles for Protection;
and then retir'd to admire my *Tableau*,
as tho' I were *God*, after the *Creation*:

How mutch it pleas'd me, to see my Goat Skin Sails
swolne with Breezes; and my Ship lift & plunge
& my brave Crew menac'd by *Cannibals*
& my larger Figurs watching from above;

but after a whil I grew troubl'd in Mind,
& my Heart pounded and I was mutch affraid;
for when I look'd, no wher cou'd I find
no Place for *Friday* in what *Friday* made;

then I was suddenly stricken & the Sun
seem'd to fly In-side my poor bursting Skull
& I stumbl'd dizzily a whil & then
fell down the Way that dead Mens Bodys fall.

XIV

Often in Feaver I would cry owt, dreaming
agayn of my Deliverance: I flee
a Mob of Fiends in humane Bodys screaming
lowder than the Sea-Shoars Foam & Sprye:

I run betwicks the Forest & the Ocean,
but burthen'd with my *Masters* Cloaths & Goods,
fatigu'd & ever slower in my Motion
until I come by that Poynt in the Woods

from which he lept owt to my Assistance
and pass it by   *nowher is my* Master
no wher Delivery   my ownly Chance
of escaping thes Fiends is to run faster

but tho' I run as tho' my Heart wou'd burst
they gain upon me   ther Cries grow lowder
in my Ears.   yet even so I durst
throw no Thing off.   Bullet   Baskets   Powder-

Horns   the Muskets which I durst not paws
to load & fire   the Pair of Pumps upon
my Feet   my Chequer'd Shirt   my Linnen Draws
either to fling off all or be undone

and I am seiz'd & flung upon my Back
environ'd by Cannibals that pin me down
whil others of them commence to chop & hack:
the Savage Face I look into is mine

no longer   Why, here I am in Bed, unhurt;
by sputtering Candle, see my wooden Chair;
upon it, folded, see my Draws & Shirt;
and all my Phrenzy vainsihes into the Nights Air . . .

Sufficiently recover'd to step owt
the following Morning, I find my Self
puzzl'd, perlex'd, *as in the deepest Doubt*;
standing with my Hand upon the Shelf

next to the Door; upon it, my *Masters* Cloathes
all lay as tho' a waiting his Return
neatly folded. I dress my Self in thes
and take up his Rifle & his Powder-Horn

his Hat & his Umbrella; and so, in his Apparell
I set owt, *as tho' to run a Way from Home*;
what Spirit made me do it, I cannot tell,
nor cou'd I say wher I desir'd to roam,

for it was not I who set owt, nor was it him,
nor was it the both of us to-gether;
I know not who it was; but, as in my Dream
of the Night befor, when I was neither

Master nor *Friday*, but I partook of each,
so it was that Morning. Whatever my Intention
I find my self walking on that Beach
to-wards that Poynt which I have earlier mention'd

and when I pass it by un-harm'd, I collaps
upon the Sand   *I lay ther in great Fear*
for a great long Time   no Savage Shapes
assail mine Eye   no screeching payns mine Ear

CODA: MR. DORRINGTON'S DISCOVERY

Ca. 1727

A herd of wild Goats having been reported
we putt 2 Boats a Shoar on an uncharted
Island neer the Mowth of the great River
Oroonoko; and there the Men discover'd
A very agreeable yong Savage,
attir'd in a Suit of Goat Skins.

When they enquir'd
merrily, *Was Tayloring his Trade*,
he answer'd them in *English: A Planter made*
this Suit for him & other ones besyde;
but now poor he, that since this Planter dy'd
must be his own Taylor.

Ask'd how he came
to dwell here, *Friday* (for that was the Name
this Planter gave him) told the Men this Tale:
That he was rais'd upon a nother Isle
some Ways from heer; and was a Caribb *Prince;*
that he had liv'd on this Isle ever since
captur'd in War-fare by a Tribe that brought him
heer for a Feast; that being what they thought him;
but he escap'd, and liv'd a great long while
with a mis-fortunate Planter from Brazil
who'd run a Grownd here. For nearly 15 Years
(rows of notched shoots became a wall of spears)
until this Planter dy'd, they liv'd together.
This Planter taught him English, et cetera.

This Evening he spoak of unseen Powers
& rav'd, delerious, for severall Howres.
Beside him lay a Goat Skin-Leather Cape
roughly cut into a Mans own Shape.
Earnestly he begg'd me to examine
this Heathen Fetisch; but an inhumane
Stench assail'd me when I try'd to do it,
for a Multitude of Worms had tunnel'd through it,
as Sappers do, to undermine a City
& left it scribbl'd with their rude *Graffiti*.
I ask'd, *Is this your own Divinity?*
All Things do say O to him, was his reply,
and gave it to me, charging me to keep
it for him safely. With that, he fell a Sleep
and I remov'd my Self, taking his Parcell,
which, as I say, reek'd like the very Devill
and was, no Doubt, the Source of his Feaver.
I gave it to my Man to throw it over-
board and now have some Hope he may recover.

B. H. Fairchild (b. 1942)

Bertram Harry Fairchild was well into his fifties before he began to excite critical attention. *The Art of the Lathe* (Alice James, 1998), a recipient of the Kingsley Tufts Poetry Award, the William Carlos Williams Award, and other prizes, preceded his next original collection, *Early Occult Memory Systems of the Lower Midwest* (W. W. Norton, 2003), winner of the National Book Critics Circle Award. In Part III of the latter volume, he describes poetry and lathework as "arts of precision." The son of a lathe machine operator, Fairchild writes: "a poet hears the syllable / before the word, a good machinist 'feels' the cut / before he measures it."

Although technique, finesse, and even perfectionism may be implied by this analogy, the poems are expansive and prosy. His plainspoken diction admits cosmopolitan references: to classical music, literature, and philosophy, but also to cinema and mid-twentieth-century pop culture. A characteristic lyric, "Beauty" (from *The Art of the Lathe*), opens with an epigraph from James Wright (1927–80). The poets share a yearning for aesthetic salvation amid blue-collar lifestyles and small-town industrial landscapes. An Edward Hopper painting, *New York Movie*, graces the jacket of *Usher* (W. W. Norton, 2009), from which "Les Passages" is drawn. The forsaken usher in Hopper's canvas seems poised to mimic the desolate cry of the pianist in Fairchild's poem.

Born in Houston, Fairchild was raised in West Texas, Oklahoma, and Kansas. He acquired bachelor's and master's degrees from the University of Kansas and a doctorate from University of Tulsa. A resident of Claremont, California, he has taught at such institutions as California State University, San Bernardino; Texas Christian University; Warren Wilson College; and the University of North Texas, and he has authored an academic study of William Blake. The title poem of *The Blue Buick: New and Selected Poems* (W. W. Norton, 2014) is an extended narrative. *An Ordinary Life* (W. W. Norton, 2023) is his most recent volume.

LES PASSAGES

The arcades ... are the residue of a dream world.
—Walter Benjamin

The piano player at Nordstrom's was crying,
and no one knew what to do. His hands were thin
and pale as the starched cuffs that seemed to hold
his wrists above the keyboard until they collapsed
and lay there among the ache of his sobs and awful
silences and the tapping of cash registers, the ocean
of small voices, the hum and click of commerce.

We all stood there, looking at him, then away,
fine linen trousers hanging from our arms,
or scent of cologne we could not afford thickening
the air, or right foot half-slipped into the new blue shoe
we would not buy, not now, not ever, and those stiff
little cries kept coming, kept tumbling across
that immense, gleaming floor into the change rooms

where men and women were gazing into mirrors
far from this strange sadness that fell clumsily
into a day rushing like all days on earth to fulfill itself,
to complete like the good postman its mission, and so
we paused in the crumbling silence until the fragile,
cautious tones of "Autumn Leaves" began to drift
through the aisles and around the glittering display cases

as if a dream, a great dream, were being dreamed again,
and the cries of an infant rose now from the other end
of the mall, cries bursting into screams and then one long
scream that spread its wings and lifted, soaring,
and we grew thoughtful and began to move about again,
searching our pockets, wallets, purses, tooled leather
handbags for something that would stop that scream.

Marilyn Hacker (b. 1942)

In her pleasingly ambitious poems, Marilyn Hacker can seem more preoccupied with formal artifice than with the traumas evoked by some of her subjects: cancer and AIDS, for example, or bigotry and antisemitism. Perhaps it would be more accurate to say that rhyme and meter, like Eros and sociability in her poems, militate against despair. Born in New York City, she attended the Bronx High School of Science and graduated from New York University before moving to London, where she worked for a time in antiquarian book sales. The poet Richard Howard (1929–2022) helped to usher her first book into print. Titled *Presentation Piece* (Viking Press, 1974), it won the National Book Award and became the Lamont Poetry Selection of the American Academy of Poets. Returning to the United States in 1976, she published her next three books with Alfred A. Knopf and began teaching at universities and editing journals, most notably the *Kenyon Review*.

Largely through sonnets, and with great panache, *Love, Death, and the Changing of the Seasons* (Arbor House, 1985) narrates a poet's experience of a lesbian love affair. *Winter Numbers* (W. W. Norton, 1994) chronicles the ravages of AIDS, the deaths of friends, and her own battle with breast cancer. The collection received the Lenore Marshall Poetry Prize and the Lambda Literary Award. Like her former mentor, Howard, Hacker has published book-length translations of French writers, specifically poets Marie Etienne (b. 1938) and Claire Malroux (b. 1925). She has spent much of her life in Paris. Her most recent editions of selected poems are *A Stranger's Mirror* (W. W. Norton, 2015) and, in the United Kingdom, *Blazons* (Carcanet Press, 2019). In 2021, she and Karthika Nair published *A Different Distance: A Renga* (Milkwood Editions), their correspondence in verse.

"Vendanges," meaning the grape harvest season, is from *Desperanto* (W. W. Norton, 2005). The poem's subject and dedicatee, Genevieve Pastre (1924–2012), was a poet and activist who greatly influenced the gay and lesbian movement in France.

VENDANGES

for Geneviève Pastre

The spiral of a story in an ear:
September, two years after the armistice
that ended the disastrous drôle de guerre.
A veteran, convinced to reenlist,
(he'd have a good pension when he retired)
your father, fifty, was a prisoner.
Morning: in the small vineyard that was his,
three sisters and their mother, out with shears
and a basket, cutting table grapes
on the slope below the Causse. This year
(you are the middle sister, seventeen)
you'd be going into hypokhâgne
at the Lycée Fénélon. A line
of men came up the hill, intent as ants,
in stained and dusty Wehrmacht uniforms.
They trudged up toward the Pas de L'Escalette.
You pictured that strait rocky pass, a site
For maquisards in ambush? When you turned,
you saw Françoise's face was white as paste.
Standing before your mother, gaunt, sunburned
and muddy, was a German officer.
He wiped his palms, schoolboyish, on his pants
and, in approximate, respectful French
requested, not demanded, food from her
(if his request could not be a command).
She cut a bunch of grapes with the knife-blade
shears, both lustrous in the morning shade.
He took it, thanked her, backed off, and diminished
to be reintegrated in the line as

it snaked up toward the Causse. Her trembling hand
clutching the sécateurs, dropped to her skirt.
Half-moons under her armpits, and a stench
of fear on the breeze. She held her shoulders braced.
"I thought of your father," she half-explained
and half-implored, looking down at the dirt.

At school, they had you tear out all of Heine's
poems from the text of German poetry.
He was a decadent; he was a Jew.
The teachers could not teach his work—but you
could read the excised pages on your own.
At least you thought that was what they implied,
and read the poems, and memorized a few
and wrote an (unread) essay when you'd finished.

In forty-five, your father, fifty-five
came home. Most of the other prisoners died.
Frost-bitten, kidneys shot, he was alive.
You were an agrégée, rebellious, grown;
barely interrogated his silence.
When he learned about the deportees,
betrayed, stripped of their rank as citizens
as if humanity could be revoked,
his story went into the family's
armoire with patched sheets, has not been aired since.
Years later, you became the one who spoke.

You are a writer in your seventies.
The spiral of a story in your ear
for once is not a story of your own.
A friend, a translator of Japanese,
showed you a just-published inédit
by a late Nippon master, who was

your sister's lover: that same dark-browed Françoise
who died of breast cancer at forty-three
after a decade in Kyoto. He
claimed she had been an "incident," naïve
enough to wait for him, enough to grieve
when he married. She made his language hers.
And his story?
                              A German officer,
half-starved, enters a garden, where a French
farm woman, all alone and almost young,
is picking fruit. In his few words of her tongue
he asks for sustenance. She cuts a bunch
of grapes for him. He remembers her
for years. He goes back after the war
(unharmed, presumably denazified)
to find her. She, of course, has disappeared.

You imagine the scene that this inferred:
the way she would have told it, with an ocean
between her and her sisters and her mother
in a noncognate language she had mastered:
fear breaching the brief maternal garden,
the writer's mind already moving past her,
filing her story, their intimacy
erased in the retelling, as the three
sisters are gone. An emblematic woman
(but with the largesse of her devotion
for the now doubly absent prisoner,
and her fear, too, now given to the invader)
remains, the icon that, somehow, he made her
into, even if he made it for her.

You don't have to imagine how she died.
You were with her. Your grief is mandatory
and quotidian. But you would rather
uncoil a spiral of the path that brought her
back to the Causse. Dawn rain left the hillside
scented with pine and sage. Wind in a hurry
to move whispered the headlines in patois:
transhumance, harvest, an absence of war
as if it were itself an absent father.
A woman in an orchard with three daughters
imagining a man somewhere who suffered,
the dust-bloomed grapes that nonetheless she proffered
to an intrusive and familiar other:
What can you do but tell someone the story?

Sydney Lea (b. 1942)

Interviewed by Brad Davis for the journal *Image*, Sydney Lea said his "profoundest influences" have been the voices he "started hearing at the dawn of memory: those of old woodsmen and women in upper New England, particularly in one region in Maine." According to Lea, those presences "were heroic in my eyes: they were embodiments of valor, perseverance, and of a quality I'd simply call sturdiness. So I decided, rightly or wrongly, that by telling stories—not theirs, but ones *like* theirs—in poetry, I might capture some of the rhythms and cadences of that beloved speech without being forced to imitate it."

This approach resulted in "The Feud" and other story-poems early in his career. In his youth, he had spent time among the residents of Washington County, Maine, where his father had family connections, and where he has maintained a camp. Lea was born in Chestnut Hill, Pennsylvania. He collected a bachelor's degree from Yale University, and then, from the same school, a PhD in comparative literature. But Vermont is the state most closely associated with his life's work. With Jay Parini, he founded the *New England Review*, published by Middlebury College, where he taught for more than a decade. From 2011 to 2015, he served as Vermont's poet laureate, and in 2021, he received the Governor's Award for Excellence in the Arts from the Vermont Arts Council.

Lea's other academic employers have included Dartmouth College, Yale, Wesleyan University, and the Vermont College of Fine Arts; he has also taught in Hungary and Switzerland. *Pursuit of a Wound* (University of Illinois Press, 2000) was a Pulitzer Prize finalist. His most recent poetry volumes are *What Shines* (2023) and *Here* (2019), both from Four Way Books. In 2021, Green Writers Press published *All Sides: Lyric and Everyday Life*, a compendium of his newspaper columns about poetry. The next year, the same press issued a third edition of *Roads Taken: Contemporary Vermont Poetry*, coedited with Chard deNiord. Lea also has written two novels: his latest, *Now Look* (Down East Books) appeared in 2024, along with an essay collection, *Such Dancing as We Can* (Humble Essayist Press).

THE FEUD

I don't know your stories. This one here
is the meanest one *I've* got or ever hope to.
Less than a year ago. Last of November,
but hot by God! I saw the Walker gang,

lugging a little buck. (A sandwich size.
It *would* be. That bunch doesn't have the patience.
I'd passed up two no smaller, and in the end
the family had no venison that fall.)

I waved to them from the porch—they just looked up—
and turned away. I try to keep good terms
with everyone, but with a crowd like that
I don't do any more than necessary.

It wasn't too much cooler back inside.
A note from my wife on the table said the heat
had driven her and the kids to the town pond beach
to sit. That made some sense. It's the last that will.

I peeked out quick through the window as the Walkers'
truck ripped past, and said out loud, "Damn fools!"
The old man, "Sanitary Jim" they call him,
at the wheel, the rifles piled between

him and "Step-and-a-Half," the crippled son.
In back, all smiles and sucking down his beer,
"Short Jim" and the deer. Now Short Jim seems all right.
To see his eyes, in fact, you'd call him shy.

He doesn't talk quite plain. Each word sounds like
a noise you'd hear from under shallow water.
I didn't give it too much thought till later,
when the wife and kids came home, and wanted to know

what in Jesus' name that awful smell was,
over the road? Turns out that Walker crew
had left their deer guts cooking in the sun.
And wasn't that just like them? Swear to God,

to leave that mess beside a neighbor's house
for stink, and for his dogs to gobble up?
And there was one thing more that puzzled me:
why wouldn't they take home that pile of guts

to feed *their* dogs? A worthless bunch—
the dogs, I mean, as well as them. You'd think
they wouldn't be above it. Every decent
dog they ever had was bullshit luck,

since every one they run is one they stole
or mooched out of the pound. You'll see them all,
hitched to one lone post, dung to the elbows,
and every time they get themselves a new one,

he'll have to fight it out until the others
either chew him up or give him up.
I guessed I'd do this feeding for them, so
I raked up all the lights into a bag

and after nightfall strewed them in their dooryard
with a note: "Since I'm not eating any deer meat,
I'd just as quick your guts rot somewhere else
as by my house." And signed my actual name.

The whole thing's clear as Judgment in my mind:
the sky was orange, the air so thick it burned
a man out of his senses. I'm the one.
And evening never seemed to cool me off,

though I'm the man whose aim is not to truck
in such a thing. I've lost most of my churching,
but don't believe in taking up with feuds.
I usually let the Good Lord have His vengeance.

Nothing any good has ever grown
out of revenge. So I was told in school
when I slapped up Lemmie Watson, because he broke
the little mill I built down on the brook.

And so I learned. I spent the afternoons
that week indoors, and I've been different since,
till this one day. Then something else took over.
There passed a week: they stove my mailbox up.

At least I don't know who in hell beside them
would have done it. I had a spare. (The Lord
knows why.) I cut a post and put it up,
and could have left the blessed fracas there,

and would have, as my wife advised me to.
And I agreed. I told myself all night,
my eyes wide open, lying there and chewing,
"Let it go." And would have, as I claim,

but two days passed, and they came hunting coons
on this side of the ridge. I heard their hounds.
(God knows what *they* were running. Hedgehogs? Skunks?
It could have been.) Out on the porch,

I heard *tick-tick*. Dog paws, and all *my* dogs
began to yap and whine. I made a light.
Shaky, thin as Satan, a docktail bitch,
a black-and-tan (almost), was looking in.

I made of her. She followed me as if
I'd owned her all my life out to the kennel.
I stuck her in the empty run that was
Old Joe's before I had to put him down.

I filled a dish with meal. She was a wolf!
The first square feed she'd had in quite a time.
My wife kept asking what I could be up to.
Likes to worry. Next day I drove clear

to Axtonbury, to the county pound.
"This dog's been hanging round my house all week.
Don't know who she belongs to." Lies, of course.
I had her collar locked in the Chevy's glovebox.

I wouldn't harm a dog unless I had to,
and figured this one stood a better show
to make out at the pound than at the Walkers'.
But the Walkers didn't know that. Driving home,

I flung the collar in their dooryard. After dark,
and spitting snow, six inches by next day,
late in December now, toward Christmas time.
Things shifted into higher gear despite me.

Or on account of me. Why not be honest?
I know that nowadays it's not the fashion
to think a person's born what he becomes;
but Sanitary Jim, his wife and family:

I never gave it too much thought but must
have figured right along that they belonged
to that great crowd of folks who *don't* belong.
Their children wear their marks right on them: speech

you hardly understand, a rock and sway
where a normal boy would take an easy stride.
And in and out of jail. If they can't find
another bunch to fight with, why, they'll fight

with one another. (Sleep with one another
too, if talk can be believed. Somehow
two homely sisters are in the mix as well.)
Short Jim beat an uncle or a cousin

—I disremember—beat him right to death.
(It's not the fashion either nowadays
to keep a violent man in jail. A month, no more,
goes by, and Short Jim's on the town again.)

But back to what I just began. The Walkers
are as bad as banty roosters, and I figured
they were meant somehow to be. Where most of us
are meant to eat one little peck of dirt,

they eat a truckload. Is it any wonder,
then, I didn't make a special point
of mixing with them? No more than I would
with any crowd that filthed itself that way.

But mix with them I did. It seemed as if
their style of working things reached up and grabbed me.
I was in the game so quick it turned my head.
The snow came on, the first big storm of winter,

that night I pulled the trick with the docktail's collar.
In the morning, barely filled, I saw their tracks
around my kennel. But *my* runs both are solid
chain-link, and the doors are padlocked shut.

They mean a thing or two to me, those dogs.
I keep the keys right on me. No one else
—no family, no good friend—can spring a dog
of mine. That way, I know they're there, or *with* me.

I'm only puzzled that they never growled. They do
as a rule. I was surely glad the Walkers hadn't
had the sense to bring along some poison.
A dog's a dog, which means he's five-eighths stomach.

Thinking on this gave me bad ideas.
But I'll get to that when time is right. For now,
I called myself a lucky fool, out loud,
and bolted both dogs shut inside their houses

nights. I judged this thing would soon blow over.
I burned a yardlight too, which I'd never done.
And that (I guessed) was the last they'd come past dark.
You know, the funny part of this whole battle

up to now, when you consider who
I'd got myself involved with, was that neither
side had come right out into the open.
The only thing I knew for sure they'd done

was leave a mess of guts out on my lawn.
The only thing for sure they knew of me—
that I returned that mess to its right home.
The mailbox and the collar and the tracks. . . .

For all we either knew, the Boss was making
visions in our eyes which, feeling righteous,
we took upon our *selves* to figure out.
And since, between the parties, I guessed *I*

had better claim to righteousness than they did,
I'm the one that—thinking back—began
to read the signs according to my will.
How many times have village hoodlums stove

a mailbox up? Or just plain village kids?
How many times, to mention what comes next,
has one old drunk shitkicker or another
raised some hell outside Ray Lawson's Auction

and Commission Sales on Friday night? And still,
I judged it was the Walkers who had slashed
all four of my new pickup's summer tires.
(Four months had passed.) And judged it quick as God.

The pickup spraddled like a hog on ice. It cost me
two hundred dollars just to run it home.
Next day I passed Short Jim as he came out
of Brandon's store and sized him up, and looked

at him: a man who'd killed another man,
but shyness in his eyes. He looked away.
And if *I'd* looked away just then. . . . Instead,
I saw a basket full of winter apples,

Baldwins mostly, full of slush and holes.
No wonder Brandon had that crop on sale!
Four cents each was asking more than enough
for winter apples still unsold in April.

If the top one hadn't had a hole as big,
almost, as half a dollar.... By God, where
would we be now? But there it was, the hole,
and I got notions. Maybe fate is notions

that you might have left alone, but took instead.
I did. I bought that apple, and another
just for show. And a box of pellets, too—
more rat pellets than I ever needed,

more than I could stuff into that hole
and still have stay enough in the rotten skin
to hold them in enough to fool a hog
that he *had* an apple. Walkers' hog, I mean.

They penned her on the far side of the road
from where that firetrap shack of theirs was built.
I didn't set right out. That apple sat
as much as seven days up on a post

of metal in the shed, where even rats
—Lord! let alone my kids—could never reach it.
And it sat inside my mind. Especially nights.
Or say it burned, the while I cooled myself

—or tried to do, with every nerve and muscle—
in bed, and said the same thing over and over:
"Nothing good will ever grow from feuds."
And just to get the apple *out* of mind,

spoke such damn foolishness you never heard:
"Old Mother Hubbard," "Stars and Stripes Forever"
(tried to get the words of one to go
along with the rhymes and rhythms of the other).

Then went down that seventh night, as if it was
another person who was going down
inside the shed (because the person I
believed I was kept up the sermon: "Nothing

any good from any feud," and so on),
picked the apple down, and put it in
my pocket, and—the moon was full—began
the uphill climb across the ridge. To Walkers'.

Stopped for breath at height of land, I turned
to see the house, where everyone was sleeping,
wondered what they dreamed, and if their dreams
were wild as mine become when moon's like that—

they say there's nothing in it, but as God
will witness me, a full moon fills my head,
asleep or not, with every bad idea.
One spring, the moon that big, a skunk came calling

in the shed, and my fool tomcat gave a rush.
The smell was worse than death. It woke me up,
if I was sleeping (I'd been trying to),
and till the dawn arrived, for hours I felt

the stink was like a judgement: every sin
from when I was a child till then flew back
and played itself again before my eyes.
High on the ridge, I felt I might reach out

and touch that moon, it was so close, but felt
that if I reached it, somehow it would burn.
It was a copper color, almost orange,
like a fire that's just beginning to take hold.

Your mind plays tricks. You live a certain while
and all the spooky stories that you read
or hear become a part of memory,
and you can't help it, grown or not, sometimes

the damnedest foolishness can haunt you. Owls,
for instance. I know owls. How many nights
do they take up outside, and I don't think
a thing about it? *That* night, though,

a pair began close by me. I'd have run,
the Devil take me, if the light had been
just one shade brighter, I'd have run right home
to get out of the woods or else to guard

the house, the wife, the kids. I don't know which.
A rat or mouse would shuffle in the leaves
and I would circle twenty yards around it.
I was close to lost until I found the brook

and waded it on down. It was half past two.
The moon kept working higher till I saw
the hog shed just across the road from Walkers' house.
There wasn't that much difference in the two.

I'm a man can't stand a mess. But they,
the boys and Sanitary Jim. . . . Well, they
can stand it. Seems that that's the way
that they *prefer* it. That hovel for the pig

was made of cardboard, chimney pipe, and wanes.
They'd driven I don't know how many sections
of ladder, side by side, into the mud
for fencing. Come the thaw each year, the ground

will heave that ladder up, and then you'll find
a pig in someone's parsnips. Anyway,
I looked the matter over, and the worry
that I'd felt about the thing that I was doing—

well, it went away. I felt as pure
as any saint or choirboy hunkered there.
I crept up on my knees and clapped the gate
(a box spring from a kid's bed) so the pig

would have a peek. I don't know why, exactly,
but I felt like watching as she took the apple
from my hand. It wouldn't do to leave it.
She just inhaled it, didn't even chew.

I backed up to the brook and watched some more,
then stepped in quick, because that poison sow
began to blow and hoot just like a bear.
The job was done. I hadn't left a track.

I don't know just what you'll make of this:
I fairly marched back up across the ridge
as if I made that climb four times a day.
The air was cold and sweet and clear, the way

it is when you can see the moon so plain.
I walked on to a beat and sang the hymns
—or sang them to myself—I'd got by heart
so many years before: "Old Rugged Cross"

and "Onward Christian Soldiers" and "Amazing
Grace," and never noticed how the cold
had numbed my feet till I was back in bed.
No one woke up. I slept two righteous hours.

You jump into a feud, and every trick's
like one more piece of kindling on the fire.
That's how I think of it, and you'll see why.
Come evening of the next day, I was sick.

You don't go paddling nighttimes in a brook
in April, and expect it's just a trick.
All night it felt like someone had a flatiron
and kept laying it between my shoulder blades.

My feet and legs were colored like old ashes.
My throat was sore enough I couldn't speak.
My wife, who didn't have a small idea
of where I'd been beside beneath the quilts,

lay it all to how I carried on.
"You've heard the old expression, 'sick with worry.'
That's what you've brought yourself, I think, from
scheming on those godforsaken Walkers." She was right,

but not the way she thought she was. In time,
there wasn't any use, I had to go
down to the clinic, twenty miles away.
You know those places: wait there half a day,

then let them pound you, scratch their heads, and scratch
some foolishness on a scrap of paper, wait
the other half while the druggist dubs around
to find the thing he's after. Come home poor.

If it was only poor that I came home!
I drove through town at fifteen miles an hour.
Swear to God I couldn't wheel it faster,
the way I was. It was a job to push

the throttle down, and I could scarcely see,
so blinked my eyes a time or two when I reached
the flat out by the pond. Above the ridge
the sky was copper-orange, and thick black smoke

was flying up to heaven, straight as string.
I thought I felt the heat. (But that was fever.)
By Jesus, that was *my* house. "Chimney fire,"
I said out loud, or loud as I could talk,

my throat ached so. The words were just a whisper,
and they sounded wrong the minute they came out.
I felt like I would die from all this sickness.
They called me "walking wounded" at the clinic:

pneumonia, but just barely, in one lung;
but now I felt my blood would burst the skin
and I'd just up and die inside that truck.
I squinched my eyes and lay the throttle on.

I meant to do some good before I died.
My wife was wrestling with a metal ladder
that had sat outside all winter, though I'd meant
to get it under cover every day.

I used it cleaning chimneys. It was stuck
in puddle ice beside the western wall.
I jumped out of the truck before it stopped,
and fell, and got back up, sweet Christ,

I tried to run, and every step I took
was like a step you take in dreams, the space
from road to house seemed fifteen thousand miles.
I stumbled to the shed and grabbed an ax

and put it to the ground to free the ladder,
but the ground just wouldn't give the damned thing up,
and every lick was like I swung the ax
from under water. I had no more force

than a kid or cripple. *My* kid, meanwhile, cried
from behind a big storm window, "Daddy? Daddy?"
It sounded like a question. I gave up
and tried to call back up to him. I couldn't.

My words were nothing more than little squeaks,
and when they did come out, they were not plain.
And so my wife began to call the boy,
"Throw something through the window and jump out!"

He threw a model boat, a book, a drumstick.
He couldn't make a crack. I flung the ax.
It missed by half a mile. I threw again
and broke a hole, and scared the boy back in.

That was the last I saw him. Like a woman
sighing, that old house huffed once and fell.
Out back, beside the kennel, our baby daughter
danced and giggled to hear the howling dogs.

I went into dead faint. And Hell could come
for all of me. And that is what has come.
Thirty years gone by since Lemmie Watson
broke my little mill of sticks and weeds

down by the brook, and I kicked the tar from him
and stayed indoors all week when school let out.
And Mrs. What's-Her-Name, I disremember,
fussing at her desk, would shake her head

and ask out loud if one small paddle wheel
was worth all this? I had to answer No.
I had to write it down, "No good can grow
from any feud." I wrote it fifty times

each afternoon. And then one afternoon
the Walker crew lay down a string of guts
across the road. . . . The part of life you think
you've got done living lies in wait like Satan.

For me, it was revenge. And what to do
right now? The house is gone, the boy, and I
believe I know just how they came to be.
But do I? Do I know what led to what

or who's to blame? This time I'll let it go.
No man can find revenge for a thing like this.
They say revenge is something for the Lord.
And let Him have it. Him, such as He is.

Marilyn Nelson (b. 1946)

In 2014, Marilyn Nelson published *How I Discovered Poetry* (Rocky Pond Books), a childhood memoir in unrhymed sonnets. It follows the artist-in-progress and her family as they relocate to various military bases with her father: a US Air Force officer and one of the last Tuskegee Airmen. Stories about this pioneering group of African American aviators inspired short narrative poems such as "Freeman Field" (given below), "Tuskegee Airfield," and "Porter"—all from an early collection, *The Homeplace* (Louisiana State University Press, 1990). The Base Commander in "Freeman Field" is Colonel Robert Selway (1902–67). The poem describes an incident that became known as the Freeman Field Mutiny.

The legend of the Tuskegee Airmen also hovers over Nelson's verse novel *American Ace* (Random House/Dial Press, 2016), one of many books she has written for children or young adults. Others include *Carver: A Life in Poems* (Boyds Mills Press/Front Street, 2001)—the winner of a Newbery Award and other honors—*A Wreath for Emmett Till* (Houghton Mifflin, 2005), which she composed as a crown of sonnets, and most recently, *Augusta Savage: The Shape of a Sculptor's Life* (Little, Brown/Christy Ottaviano Books, 2022). For adult readers of poetry, Nelson has published such collections as *The Meeting House* (Antrim House, 2016), *The Thirteenth Month* (Oberlin College Press, 2005), and *The Fields of Praise: New and Selected Poems* (Louisiana State University Press, 1997). The latter volume earned the Lenore Marshall Poetry Prize from the American Academy of Poets, the Poets' Prize, and the PEN Winship Award (now known as the PEN New England Award). As with two of her other books, it was a finalist for the National Book Award.

Born in Cleveland, Ohio, Nelson graduated from the University of California, Davis, and completed graduate studies at the University of Pennsylvania and the University of Minnesota before teaching at the University of Connecticut as a professor of English. She was Connecticut's poet laureate from 2001 to 2006. Already a recipient of the Ruth Lilly Poetry Prize and the Frost Medal, in 2022 she collected the Wallace Stevens Award for lifetime achievement.

THE BALLAD OF AUNT GENEVA

Geneva was the wild one.
Geneva was a tart.
Geneva met a blue-eyed boy
and gave away her heart.

Geneva ran a roadhouse.
Geneva wasn't sent
to college like the others:
Pomp's pride her punishment.

She cooked out on the river,
watching the shore slide by,
her lips pursed into hardness,
her deep-set brown eyes dry.

They say she killed a woman
over a good black man
by braining the jealous heifer
with an iron frying pan.

They say, when she was eighty,
she got up late at night
and sneaked her old, white lover in
to make love, and to fight.

First, they heard the tell-tale
singing of the springs,
then Geneva's voice rang out:
I need to buy some things,

So next time, bring more money.
And bring more moxie, too.
I ain't got no time to waste
on limp white mens like you.

Oh yeah? Well, Mister White Man,
it sure might be stone-white,
but my thing's white as it is.
And you know damn well I'm right.

Now listen: take your heart pills
and pay the doctor mind.
If you up and die on me,
I'll whip your white behind.

They tiptoed through the parlor
On heavy, time-slowed feet.
She watched him, from her front door,
walk down in the dawnlit street.

Geneva was the wild one.
Geneva was a tart.
Geneva met a blue-eyed boy
and gave away her heart.

FREEMAN FIELD

For Edward Wilson Woodward, Captain USAF (ret.)
and the 101 of the 477th

It was a cool evening
in the middle of April.
The 477th, the only Negro
bombardier group in the Air Corps,
had just been transferred
to Freeman Field.

Some of the guys
said they were hungry
and left to find food.
The others went on
playing bridge,
mending socks,
writing letters home.

A few minutes later
the hungry guys came back,
still hungry.
We're under arrest.

The others thought they were kidding.

The next morning
the Base Commander
issued new regulations:
Negro officers were assigned
to the NCO Club;
white officers were assigned
to the Officers' Club.

The Base Commander,
who had deliberately busted
an entire Negro outfit
so he wouldn't have to be
their flight-leader in combat,
was a graduate of West Point.

He issued a statement:
If we do not allow
Negro and white officers to mix,
the accident rate
will go down two
and two-tenths
percent.

Sixty-one Negro officers
were ordered to report
one by one
to his office.
Lieutenant, have you read the regulations?
Sign here if you have read and understood.

Sixty-one Negro officers
refused to sign.
A man of your intelligence
must be able to recognize
the dangers of fraternization.

They refused to sign.
This is an order:
Sign the document.

They refused to sign.
This is a direct order!
You will sign the document!

Six cargo planes were called in;
pilots, navigators, and bombardiers
were shoved on board and flown
to Goodman Field, Kentucky.

Across the river
was Fort Knox.
The sixty-one
had grown by now
to one hundred and one
American fliers trained
to fight Nazis.
They were confined
to the BOQ
under guard
of armed MPs.

By night, searchlights watched
every window. By daylight
the men leaned in the windows
to smoke, watching
the German POWs pump gas,
wash windshields
and laugh
at the motorpool
across the street.

Robert B. Shaw (b. 1947)

Robert Burns Shaw's facility with blank verse is evident not only in the two poems given here, but also in the keen empirical insights that permeate his *Blank Verse: A Guide to Its History and Use* (Ohio University Press, 2007), winner of the Robert Fitzgerald Prosody Award. Other narrative specimens—in blank verse or otherwise—abound in *What Remains to Be Said: New and Collected Poems* (Pinyon Publishing, 2022).

Born in Philadelphia, and now a professor emeritus at Mount Holyoke College, Shaw is the recipient of the Hollis Summer Prize for *Solving for X* (Ohio University Press, 2002) and the Poets' Prize for *Aromatics* (Pinyon Publishing, 2011). He has been awarded, among other literary honors, fellowships from the National Endowment for the Arts and the Ingram Merrill Foundation. Apart from his study of blank verse, Shaw authored *The Call of God: The Theme of Vocation in the Poetry of Donne and Herbert* (Cowley Publications, 1981). He got his bachelor's degree from Harvard University, where he studied with Robert Fitzgerald and Robert Lowell, and a PhD from Yale University.

BIRTH OF A CRITICAL SPIRIT

for Michael Johnston

Ten years old, on his annual summer visit,
he noticed how much easier, on the whole,
it was to be grandson, nephew—not a son.
Uncle and Aunt, married as much to the farm
as to each other, left him alone. Grandfather
napped in the parlor under a newspaper tent.
Grandmother kept to the kitchen, busy with dough.
He didn't feel unwanted, only free.
He ran in the far pasture dodging cowflops
and mildly annoying cows, or fished for minnows.
Mostly he sat against the springhouse wall,
its boards black with damp and cool to his back,
reading his books on lower forms of life.

A memorable summer: some weeks before,
he had been fitted for his first eyeglasses.
Types of fodder, once all a wash of green,
now took bows, here timothy, there alfalfa.
Print lay flat on the page, its glimmer gone.
He read unmindful of time, and came to supper
each night equipped with queasy natural facts:
the flatworm's way of growing back a head
no matter how many times you cut it off;
the flounder's migrating eyes, the lady scorpion
capping a tryst by gobbling up her mate.
The seagull's regurgitant feeding of its chicks . . .
"Please, not at the table." That was his aunt.
His uncle, though, would hasten to mend matters:
"That's all right, tell us more about the scorpions."
Grandfather grinned, or came as close to grinning

as a midwestern patriarch might. Grandmother
managed a quick retreat by stacking plates
and soon from the kitchen a soapy clatter arose.

Was it that night it occurred to him that *they*
were in the way of being specimens?—
Aunt, dabbing a napkin at an upper
lip that never needed such attentions,
Uncle, tilting back in a creaky chair,
lacing satisfied thumbs in frayed suspenders.
How do you put a finger on such a moment?
Enough to say, sitting there, one summer evening,
hearing the buzz and thud behind his back
of June bugs stupidly battering the screen,
rubbing a darned spot on the table cloth
as if he were a beginner reading Braille,
he swore himself to singularity,
detachment, living in the light of science.
His insights would be his, not other men's.
Looking up, he saw his people stirring
their coffee, smiling at him through the lens.

HIDE-AND-SEEK

Under the table was no good. The cloth
hung down at most halfway. Behind the sofa
two friends were already huddled. She could hear
her brother on the back porch counting down—
". . . three, two, one"—and just before
his bellowed "Ready or not, here I come"
she dove into the closet under the stairs.
Not much bigger than a telephone booth
and with a ceiling sloping to the floor,
it was a catch-all bin for hanging coats
(or slickers, once the coats were coffined up
in cedar for the summer) and for stowing
items lacking obvious spots to be in.
The vacuum cleaner and the croquet set
claimed much of the floor space. There were a few
stacks of the magazines her mother meant
to read sometime before they were thrown out.
She sat down quietly on one of these
and let her eyes grow more used to the dark.

It wasn't totally dark in any case:
there was a glowing finger's-width between
door and floorboard, and from the keyhole
an even brighter wizard's wand was jabbed,
searching into the farthest reach of shadow,
solid-looking, pencil-thin, unfaltering,
tempting to put a fist around except
it looked white hot enough to leave a brand
on any flesh it touched. (She knew it wouldn't,
but kept hands off it anyway.) She stared
at jumpy, moiling motes of dust it harried

out of invisibility and held
in its suspended corridor for inspection.
Once she had asked her mother, "Where does dust
come from?" and her mother, dusting, said,
"I declare, I think it comes from you."
Could it be true? She peered at the minute
and witless midair antics. Then she felt an itch,
and quietly, because by now she heard
footsteps and giggles of others being found,
she rubbed mosquito lumps around her ankle.

Under her pumicing fingers she could feel
smidgens of something crumbing from the surface—
the summer's grime? Or her own skin, somehow
more friable than she'd assumed? The thought
of turning into dust by merely rubbing
herself away, being her own eraser,
grain by grain becoming part and parcel
of the unresting flurry she now gaped at,
gripped her. For the lit-up mites she saw
there were a multitude she couldn't see:
they were what the dark air touching her
all over now was full of. When her brother
finally got wise and crept up soundlessly
to the shut door and slid a gleeful thumb
over the keyhole, terror tripped a switch
deep in her throat, and the scream she came
bursting into the light with scared him, too.
So when she reached out to him, he was rattled,
said not to be silly, slapped her wrist,
and ran away, yelling that she was It.

Daniel Mark Epstein (b. 1948)

Born in Washington, DC, Daniel Mark Epstein began publishing poetry books in the 1970s, also writing plays that ran in regional theater and off Broadway. A volume of his collected poems is forthcoming from Louisiana University Press, which rendered the same service to John Crowe Ransom and Robert Penn Warren—two poets famously associated with Epstein's alma mater, Kenyon College. At Kenyon, he has been an affiliated scholar in American studies. The liberal arts college has granted him an honorary doctorate, and in 2023 announced the acquisition of his writerly correspondence.

Literary references abound in his poetry, and they often provide a subject. "A Dream," which appears in the Winter 2023 issue of *Narrative* magazine, was occasioned by a signed copy of *The March of Literature* (1938), by Ford Madox Ford. As seen in the following two poems, Epstein handles classical themes and topics in an unobtrusive way, in lines less startling than functional, advancing to an inspired coda. "The Ferryman" retells a story by the Anglo-Irish fabulist and playwright Lord Dunsany (1878–1957). That poem, and "Helen," can be found in Epstein's 1995 collection, *The Boy in the Well and Other Poems* (Overlook Press).

In addition to poetry, and book-length translations from Plautus and Euripides, Epstein has published volumes of essays and short stories. He is perhaps best known for his biographies. These include, among others, *The Ballad of Bob Dylan: A Portrait* (HarperCollins, 2011), *Lincoln and Whitman: Parallel Lives in Civil War Washington* (Random House, 2004), and *What My Lips Have Kissed: The Loves and Love Poems of Edna St. Vincent Millay* (Henry Holt, 2001). In 2022, Yale University Press published his edition of Millay's diaries, *Rapture and Melancholy*. Epstein has been honored with the Prix de Rome and the Academy Award for Lifetime Achievement, both from the American Academy and Institute of Arts and Letters.

THE FERRYMAN

(after a tale of Dunsany)

For him it was not a matter of years
Or even centuries, but wide floods of time
And the ancient heaviness and ache
In his corded arms that had become
Part of the grand scheme the gods had made.
Now if they should send a cruel head wind
How could it help or hinder or change things
Except to divide all time in his memory
Into two equal portions? So evenly grey
Everything looked where he rowed, if any
Radiance flickered a moment among the dead,
On the face of a Cleopatra or a Bernhardt,
The ferryman never would have noticed it.

Yet he did notice and thought it strange
When the dead began arriving in such numbers:
They come in hundreds, sometimes thousands now
Who used to come in dozens, long ago.
His job was not to count, it was to row.
But then for a long time there was no traffic,
And this is uncommon, he thought, for the gods
To send no one down from earth for a decade—
Though gods in their wisdom know what's best.

Then one man walked the pier. His little shade
Sat shivering on the skiff as it pushed off.
Only one passenger: the gods know best.
The weary ferryman rowed on and on
And the river sighed the way Grief in the dawn

Of ages moaned and sighed among her sisters,
A song that could not die like the echoes
Of human sorrow failing on the earth,
Though it was old as Time and Charon's pain.

From the slow river the boat loomed to the coast
Of Hades. The lone passenger stepped ashore
As Charon turned his boat toward the world.
"But wait, I am the last," said the new ghost
Alarmed by Charon's face against the sky—
For no one had ever made him smile before,
No one had ever seen the ferryman cry.

HELEN

"Tell us a love story,"
Pleaded the class in chorus.
"Our lessons are all done,
Now don't lecture or bore us,"

They prattled, except for one,
Helen, whose gaze looked lost
In the maze of willow branches,
The girl the boys liked most

For the faraway blue of her eyes
And brown hair straight as rain.
"Tell us a love story, please,"
They begged the teacher again.

He frowned and longed for the bell,
Saying "All the love stories I know
End in heartache, or death—"
Then Helen, from the back row

Called at last from her daydream
In the voice of an innocent lover,
"Tell us a love story anyway
And stop before it is over."

Michael Donaghy (1954–2004)

If Michael Donaghy's untimely death was mourned more loudly in Great Britain and Ireland than in the United States, it is because this Bronx, New York, native had by then risen to the top tier of formally inclined poets in his adopted country of England. But part of this grief, vocalized by poets such as Don Paterson, Sean O'Brien, Glyn Maxwell, and David Wheatley, surely had to do with the loss of a virtuosic wit that coaxed musicality from technical precision. After graduate study in English at the University of Chicago, where Donaghy edited the *Chicago Review*, he moved to London in 1985. There he swiftly earned acclaim both as a poet and as a performer of Irish traditional music. In his lifetime, he published three full collections and *Dances Learned Last Night: Poems 1975–1995* (Picador, 2000). *Safest* (Picador, 2006) appeared posthumously, as did his *Collected Poems* and *The Shape of the Dance: Interviews and Digressions*, both published by Picador in 2009.

The title of the first entry—a sestina—refers to a trickster figure in Yoruba mythology. In the West, the term was popularized by Henry Louis Gates Jr.'s *The Signifying Monkey: A Theory of Afro-American Literary Criticism* (Oxford University Press, 1988).

SIGNIFYIN' MONKEY

"Never write a check with your mouth your ass can't cash."
—Zach Newton

O.K. I'll tell it, but only if you buy lunch.
One summer I worked nights for Vigil-Guard,
the Chicago security firm. The work was easy:
sitting. And close to home. Ten minutes on the train.
And every night I passed the same fluorescent sign
somewhere in Chinatown: FIGHTER MONKEY.

I paid it no mind. It was the year of the monkey.
I thought I'd try it out one day for lunch.
Risky, I figured, but it's always a good sign
If the sign's in English. I wasn't made chief guard
for nothing, you know. It takes a week to train
on half pay so don't think it's all that easy.
Security's an art. I just make it *look* easy,
like the day I walked home past Fighter Monkey.
Looking back, I wish I'd caught that train,
but I was after a cheap pork feng shui lunch.
Something out front put me on my guard,
though, something about that Day-Glo sign,
the smell, and the cages in the windows, and no sign
of a menu anywhere, which made me a little uneasy,
when out steps this white guy built like a bodyguard
wearing a T-shirt showing a shrieking monkey.
He just stands there, chin out. "Still serving lunch?"
I ask. "This is no restaurant," he says. "I train
animals"—He's got this tight whisper—"I train
Barbary Apes using American Sign
Language." O.K. I figure he's out to lunch,

a potential situation. "Take it easy,"
I tell him. "I made a mistake. *You* train monkeys . . .
I represent a firm called Vigil-Guard."

Turns out he once trained dogs for Vigil-Guard.
And he pays me there and then to help him train
one of his babies, a kind of Rottweiler monkey
that took her orders and talked back in Sign.
I swear she must have weighed forty pounds easy.
And teeth! She could have had me for lunch.
Then he hauls out this heavy, padded armguard.
"Put that on," he says. "This part is safe and easy.
She's going to come at you like a freight train.
Freeze." I remember he laughed as he made the sign.
The asshole. Lost a thumb to his own monkey.

It's easy. Look, he'd been her only trainer.
Guard or no guard, he'd signed "I'm lunch."
The blood! Of course they had to shoot the monkey.

BLACK ICE AND RAIN

Psalms 6:6

Can I come in? I saw you slip away.
Hors d'oeuvres depress you, don't they? They do me.
And cocktails, jokes . . . such dutiful abandon.
Where the faithful observe immovable feasts
— boat races, birthdays, marriages, martyrdoms —
we're summoned to our lonely ceremonies any time:
B minor, the moldiness of an old encyclopedia,
the tinny sun snapping off the playground swings,
these are, though we can't know this, scheduled
to arrive that minute of the hour, hour of the day,
day of every year. Again, regular as brickwork,
comes the time the nurse jots on your chart
before she pulls the sheet across your face. Just so,
the past falls open anywhere — even sitting here with you.

Sorry. You remind me of a girl I knew.
I met her at a party much like this, but younger, louder,
the bass so fat, the night so sticky you could drown.
We shouted art at each other over soul
and cold beer in the crowded kitchen and I, at least,
was halfway to a kiss when she slipped
her arm around her friend.
I worked at liking him, and it took work,
and it never got any easier being harmless,
but we danced that night like a three-way game of chess
and sang to Curtis Mayfield pumped so loud
that when I drove them home they could hardly
whisper to invite me up.

Their black walls smirked with Jesus on black velvet
— Jesus, Elvis, Mexican skeletons, big-eyed Virgins,
Rodin's hands clasped in chocolate prayer —
an attitude of decor, not like this room of yours.
A bottle opened — tequila with a cringe of worm —
and she watched me.
Lighting a meltdown of Paschal candles,
she watched me. He poured the drinks rasping
We're seriously into cultural detritus. At which, at last,
she smiled. Ice cubes cracked. The worm sank in my glass.
And all that long year we were joined at the hip.

I never heard them laugh. They had,
instead, this tic of scratching quotes in the air —
like frightened mimes inside their box of style,
that first class carriage from whose bright window
I watched the suburbs of my life recede.
    Exactly one year on she let me kiss her — once —
her mouth wine-chilled, my tongue a clumsy guest,
and after that the invitations dwindled.
By Christmas we were strangers. It was chance
I heard about the crash. He died at once.
Black ice and rain, they said. No news of her.

I can't remember why I didn't write.
Perhaps I thought she'd sold the flat and left.

Some nights midway to sleep I'm six years old.
Downstairs it's New Year's Eve. Drink and shrieks.
But my mother's lit the luminous plastic Jesus
to watch me through the night, which is why
I've got my pillow wrapped around my head.
I never heard the door. And when she speaks,
her thick-tongued anger rearing like a beast,

I feel my hot piss spreading through the sheets.
But when I wake, grown up, it's only sweat.
But if I dream, I bleed. A briar crown,
a fist prised open wide, a steadied nail,
a hammer swinging down — the past falls open
anywhere . . .
                    Ash Wednesday evening.
Driving by, I saw her lights were on.
I noticed both their names still on the buzzer
and when I rang I heard their voice. *Come in —*
    her nose was broken, her front teeth gone,
a rosary was twisted round her fists —
        — Come in. I've been saying a novena.
Inside, each crucifix and candle shone
transfigured in her chrysalis of grief.
She spoke about the crash, how she'd been driving,
how they had to cut her from the wreck . . .
and then she slipped and called me by his name.

Of those next hours I remember most
the silences between her sobs, the rain
against the skylight slowly weakening
to silence, silence brimming into sleep and dawn.
Then, having lain at last all night beside her,
having searched at last that black-walled room,
the last unopened chamber of my heart,
and found there neither pity nor desire
but an assortment of religious kitsch,
I inched my arm from under her and left.

    Since then, the calmest voice contains her cry
just within the range of human hearing
and where I've hoped to hear my name gasped out

from cradle, love bed, death bed, there instead
I catch her voice, her broken lisp, his name.
Since then, each night contains all others,
nested mirror-within-mirror, stretching back from then
to here and now, this party, this room, this bed,
where, in another life, we might have kissed.
Thank you, friend, for showing me your things —
you have exquisite taste — but let's rejoin your guests
who must by now be wondering where you've gone.

Dana Gioia (b. 1950)

Dana Gioia was born in Hawthorne, California, just outside Los Angeles. His mother was Mexican American, his father of Sicilian origin. Both parents worked full time, sometimes at more than one job. The family home was crammed with literature in many languages, musical scores, and classical record albums, the legacy of a maternal uncle who had died in a plane crash.

As a youth, he rapidly absorbed this heritage and sought out more arts and cultural experiences in the LA area. He earned a BA and an MBA from Stanford, and an MA in comparative literature from Harvard, taking classes from the poets Robert Fitzgerald and Elizabeth Bishop—both of whom would figure in *Studying with Miss Bishop: Memoirs from a Young Writer's Life* (Paul Dry Books, 2021). He worked at General Foods for fifteen years, rising to the position of vice president of marketing, and dispatching poems and essays at night. His third full collection of poems, *Interrogations at Noon* (Graywolf Press, 2001), won the American Book Award. *Can Poetry Matter?* (Graywolf Press, 1992) grew from a widely discussed essay he published in *The Atlantic*.

In 2003, President George W. Bush appointed Gioia the ninth chair of the National Endowment for the Arts. In this capacity, he launched enduring national programs. He taught at the University of Southern California before serving as the state's poet laureate from 2015 to 2018. His most recent poetry collections are *Meet Me at the Lighthouse* (Graywolf Press, 2023) and *99 Poems: New and Selected* (Graywolf Press, 2016), winner of the Poets' Prize. He has also published volumes of translations and libretti. Through his critical essay collections, the textbooks he has edited for students of literature, and his cofounding of poetry conferences, Gioia has helped to bring order and method to the contemporary literary landscape. And yet his poems are anything but didactic. Seldom have clarity and mystery been so conjoined as in a Gioia poem. It is an achievement entirely commensurate with the aims of one who has spoken and written about "Poetry and the Catholic Imagination" and "Poetry as Enchantment." The latter is the title of an essay collection he published with Paul Dry Books in 2024. That year, the same press issued his love letter to opera, *Weep, Shudder, Die*, which promotes the librettist's role as central to composition and performance.

COUNTING THE CHILDREN

I.

"This must have been her bedroom, Mr. Choi.
It's hard to tell. The only other time
I came back here was when I found her body."

Neither of us belonged there. She lived next door.
I was the accountant sent out by the State
To take an inventory of the house.

When someone wealthy dies without a will,
The court sends me to audit the estate.
They know that strangers trust a man who listens.

The neighbor led me down an unlit hall.
We came up to a double door and stopped.
She whispered as if someone else were near.

"She used to wander around town at night
And rifle through the trash. We all knew that.
But what we didn't know about was *them*."

She stepped inside and fumbled for a switch.
It didn't work, but light leaked through the curtains.
"Come in," she said. "I want to show you hell."

I walked into a room of wooden shelves
Stretching from floor to ceiling, wall to wall,
With smaller shelves arranged along the center.

A crowd of faces looked up silently.
Shoulder to shoulder, standing all in rows,
Hundreds of dolls were lining every wall.

Not a collection anyone would want—
Just ordinary dolls salvaged from the trash
With dozens of each kind all set together.

Some battered, others missing arms and legs,
Shelf after shelf of the same dusty stare
As if despair could be assuaged by order.

They looked like sisters huddling in the dark,
Forgotten brides abandoned at the altar,
Their veils turned yellow, dresses stiff and soiled.

Not just a collection anyone would want—
Just ordinary dolls salvaged from the trash
With dozens of each kind all set together.

Some battered, others missing arms and legs,
Shelf after shelf of the same dusty stare
As if despair could be assuaged by order.

They looked like sisters huddling in the dark,
Forgotten brides abandoned at the altar,
Their veils turned yellow, dresses stiff and soiled.

Rows of discarded little girls and babies—
Some naked, others dressed for play—they wore
Whatever lives their owners left them in.

Where were the children who promised them love?
The small, caressing hands, the lips which whispered
Secrets in the dark? Once they were woken,

Each by name. Now they have become each other—
Anonymous except for injury,
The beautiful and headless side by side.

Was this where all lost childhoods go? These dim
Abandoned rooms, these crude arrangements staged
For settled dust and shadow, left to prove

That all affection is outgrown, or show
The uniformity of our desire?
How dismal someone else's joy can be.

I stood between the speechless shelves and knew
Dust has a million lives, the heart has one.
I turned away and started my report.

II.

That night I dreamt of working on a ledger,
A book so large it stretched across my desk,
Thousands of numbers running down each page.

I knew I had to settle the account,
Yet as I tried to calculate the total,
The numbers started slipping down the page,

Suddenly breaking up like Scrabble letters
Brushed into a box to end a game,
Each strained-for word uncoupled back to nil.

But as I tried to add them back together
And hold each number on the thin green line
Where it belonged, I realized that now

Nothing I did would ever fit together.
In my hands even 2 + 2 + 2
No longer equaled anything at all.

And then I saw my father there beside me.
He asked me why I couldn't find the sum.
He held my daughter crying in his arms.

My family stood behind him in a row,
Uncles and aunts, cousins I'd never seen,
My grandparents from China and their parents,

All of my family, living and dead,
A line that stretched as far as I could see.
Even the strangers called to me by name.

And now I saw I wasn't at my desk
But working on the coffin of my daughter,
And she would die unless I found the sum.

But I had lost too many of the numbers.
They tumbled to the floor and blazed on fire.
I saw the dolls then—screaming in the flames.

III.

When I awoke, I sat up straight in bed.
The sweaty sheet was twisted in my hands.
My heart was pounding. Had I really screamed?

But no, my wife was still asleep beside me.
I got up quietly and found my robe,
Knowing I couldn't fall asleep again.

Then groping down the unlit hall, I saw
A soft-edged light beneath my daughter's door.
It was the night-light plugged in by her bed.

And I remembered when she was a baby,
How often I would get up in the night
And creep into that room to watch her sleep.

I never told my wife how many times
I came to check each night—or that I was
Always afraid of what I might discover.

I felt so helpless standing by her crib,
Watching the quiet motions of her breath
In the half-darkness of the faint night-light.

How delicate this vessel in our care,
This gentle soul we summoned to the world,
A life we treasured but could not protect.

This was the terror I could not confess—
Not even to my wife—and it was the joy
My daughter had no words to understand.

So standing at my pointless watch each night
In the bare nursery we had improvised,
I learned the loneliness that we call love.

IV.

But I gave up those vigils years ago.
My daughter's seven now, and I don't worry—
At least no more than any father does.

But waking up last night after the dream,
Trembling in the hall, looking at her door,
I let myself be drawn into her room.

She was asleep—the blankets softly rising
And falling with each breath, the faint light tracing
The sleek unfoldings of her long black hair.

Then suddenly I felt myself go numb.
And though you won't believe that an accountant
Can have a vision, I will tell you mine.

Each of us thinks our own child beautiful,
But watching her and marveling at the sheer
Smoothness of skin without a scar or blemish,

I saw beyond my daughter to all children,
And, though elated, still I felt confused
Because I wondered why I never sensed

That thrill of joy when looking at adults
No matter how refined or beautiful,
Why lust or envy always intervened.

There is no *tabula rasa* for the soul.
Each spirit, be it infant, bird or flower,
Comes to the world perfected and complete,

And only time proves its unraveling.
But I'm digressing from my point, my vision.
What I meant to ask is merely this:

What if completion comes only in beginnings?
The naked tree exploding into flower?
And all our prim assumptions about time

Prove wrong? What if we cannot read the future
Because our destiny moves back in time,
And only memory speaks prophetically?

We long for immortality, a soul
To rise up flaming from the body's dust.
I know that it exists. I felt it there,

Perfect and eternal in the way
That only numbers are, intangible but real,
Infinitely divisible yet whole.

But we do not possess it in ourselves.
We die, and it abides, and we are one
With all our ancestors, while it divides

Over and over, common to us all,
The ancient face returning in the child,
The distant arms embracing us, the salt

Of our blind origins filling our veins.
I stood confused beside my daughter's bed
Surprised to find the room around me dim.

Then glancing at the bookshelf in the corner,
I saw she'd lined her dolls up in a row.
Three little girls were sitting in the dark.

Their sharp glass eyes surveyed me with contempt.
They recognized me only as a rival,
The one whose world would keep no place for them.

I felt like holding them tight in my arms,
Promising I would never let them go,
But they would trust no promises of mine.

I feared that if I touched one, it would scream.

HAUNTED

"I don't believe in ghosts," he said. "Such nonsense.
But years ago I actually saw one."
He seemed quite serious, and so I asked.

It happened almost forty years ago.
The world was different then—not just for ghosts—
slower, less frantic. You're too young to know
life without cell phones, laptops, satellite.
You didn't bring the world with you everywhere.
Out in the country, you were quite alone.

I was in love with Mara then, if love
is the right word for that particular
delusion. We were young. We thought we could
create a life made only of peak moments.
We laughed. We drank. We argued and made love.
Our battles were Homeric—not Homer's heroes
but his gods, petty, arrogant Olympians
thundering in their egotistic rage.

Mara was brilliant, beautiful, refined.
She'd walk into a room dressed for the evening,
and I would lose a breath. She seemed to shine
as movie stars shine, made only of light.
And did I mention she was rich? And cruel?

Do you know what it's like to be in love
with someone bad? Not simply bad for you,
but slightly evil? You have to decide
either to be the victim or accomplice.
I'm not the victim type. That's what she liked.

I envied her sublime self-confidence.
She could freeze someone with a single sentence,
too witty to be rude but deeply wounding,
impossible to deflect or forget.
If I sound slightly bitter, please understand,
it is myself I now despise, not Mara.
She simply recognized what I desired.

Her uncle owned a house up in the Berkshires,
not just a summer house, a country manor,
three stories high with attics, basement, turrets,
surrounded by great lawns and sunken gardens,
hundreds of wooded acres whispering wealth.

We came up for a few days in late autumn,
driving through bare woods under a gray sky,
the landscape still, no birds, barely a breeze,
hushed as the hour after heavy snowfall.

The house had been vacated since September.
I had imagined it as dark and gothic,
cloaked in shadow like something out of Lovecraft,
but the decor was opulently cozy,
a proper refuge for a Robber Baron,
stuffed with *objets* to certify his status,
though slightly shabby from a century's use.

The art was grand, authentic, second rate.
Florentine bronzes, Belgian tapestries,
carved stonework pried from bankrupt Tudor manors,
and landscapes by the minor Barbizons.
Nothing quite fit together. I suspect
sumptuous excess was the desired effect,
a joyful shout to celebrate success—

good taste be damned—let's just indulge ourselves
and revel like a child who greets his playmates
by emptying his toy chest on the floor.
What fun is wealth if no one notices?
Mara seemed to think so. What did I know?
I'd never seen the rich up close before.

While Mara showered, I explored the cellars,
searching a maze of mildewed storage rooms
until I found a faux medieval door,
flanked by a pair of somber wooden saints.
You should have seen the wine her uncle owned—
six vaulted rooms stocked with the great estates,
bin after bin of legendary names,
Château Margaux, Latour, Lafite-Rothschild,
a prodigal accumulation formed
on such a scale he could have entertained
Napoleon and half his *Grande Armée*.

I chose two bottles of pre-war Petrus
That probably cost as much as my month's rent.
Clutching their dusty necks, I closed the door,
And told the saints, "I could get used to this."
They didn't condescend to give an answer.

That night we drank in the high paneled library,
a great inferno blazing in the fireplace.
Naked Diana stood in tapestry
above us on the wall. Below her, Mara,
stylishly overdressed, refilled our glasses.

Resplendently the room reminded us
that beauty always bears a heavy price.
White tiger skins lay stretched across the floor.
Martyred Sebastian twisted on a pedestal.
Even the dusty books were bound in leather.

Mara loved having me as audience.
She sat there, half illumined by the fire
and half in shadow, spinning out long stories.
They were as fine as anything in books.
No, they were better because they were true.

She was a connoisseur of *Schadenfreude*
and was especially wicked in describing
her former lovers—imitating them,
cataloguing their signature stupidities,
and relishing their subsequent misfortunes.
(I'm surely in her repertory now.)

At first I was embarrassed by her candor.
I felt more like a confidant than lover,
but gradually I understood the motive—
even she needed someone to impress.
Life was a contest. Mara was a champion.
What good was winning if no one noticed?

Of course, that night we drank too much and argued.
She strode off, slamming doors theatrically.
I sat still, slowly finishing my drink,
feigning indifference—just as she would have—
and then went to the other wing to sleep.
Let her find me, I thought. Let her apologize.
She won't like sleeping in this house alone.

The room was cold, and I was too annoyed
to fall asleep. I stretched out on the bed,
still wearing all my clothes, and tried to read.
Believe it or not, the book was Shakespeare's sonnets.
What sweeter text for wounded vanity?
Farewell, thou art too dear for my possessing.
I'd found an old edition in the library,
and from sheer spitefulness I'd stolen it.
That night each poem seemed written just for me.
What is your substance, whereof are you made,
That millions of strange shadows on you tend?

I hope this explanation makes it clear
I wasn't sleeping when I saw her enter—
Mara, I thought, mad at being ignored,
coming to make a scene. But, no, it was
a handsome woman in her early forties.
I thought she might have been a housekeeper
come in from town to check up on the place,
but why was she so elegantly dressed?

I started to explain why I was there.
She didn't seem to hear and turned away.
Could she be deaf? I didn't want to scare her.
Something was wrong. I couldn't see her clearly.
She seemed at once herself and her own reflection
shimmering on the surface of clear water
where fleeting shadows twisted in the depths.

I found it hard admitting what I saw.
She seemed to be a ghost, though that sounds crazy.
Oddly, I wasn't scared—just full of wonder,
watching this thing I knew could not exist,
this woman standing by her dressing table,

translucent, insubstantial, but still there,
and utterly oblivious of me.
First to be haunted, then to be ignored!

Her back toward me, she started to undress.
Now I was panicked and embarrassed both.
I spoke much louder. She made no response.
Now wearing only a long silk chemise,
she turned toward me, still strangely indistinct,
the fabric undulating, as if alive.
I felt her eyes appraise me, and I sat
half paralyzed as she approached the bed.

Here I was face to face with a dead soul,
some entity regathered from the dust,
returned like Lazarus from the silent tomb,
whose mere existence, right before my eyes,
confounded my belief there could not be
an afterlife. Think what this meeting represented—
a skeptic witnessing the unexplained.

I could have learned the secrets of the dead
if there are any secrets, which I doubt.
So how did I address this revenant,
this traveler from the undiscovered country,
who stared at me with dark, unblinking eyes?
I caught my breath, got on my feet, and said—
nothing at all. The words stuck in my throat.

We stood there face to face, inches apart.
Her pale skin shined like a window catching sunlight,
both bright and clear, but chilling to the touch.
She stared at me with undisguised contempt,
and then she whispered, almost in a hiss,

"You don't belong here. No, you don't belong here."
She slowly reached to touch me, and I ran
leaving behind both Shakespeare and my shoes.

Mara was still awake when I arrived.
The lamp was on. The fireplace ablaze.
And she stretched naked under satin sheets.
(She couldn't resist striking pinup poses.)
"So, you've come back?" she yawned with mock ennui,
then added with a smirk, "You weren't gone long."
I didn't say a word of what I'd seen.

We used to sleep in one another's arms,
our two slim bodies interlaced like hands.
That night I held her, feeling our hearts beat—
first hers, then mine—always out of sync,
and in the dark I thought, *I don't belong here,*
I don't belong here. Slipping out of bed,
I quickly dressed, and what I couldn't wear
I left behind—the clothes, the books, the camera,
no longer mine. What a surprise to first feel
the liberations of divestiture.

I moved with such new lightness down the stairs,
watched by mute saints and marble goddesses.
Then out the door. I closed it quietly.
The lock clicked shut. Good-bye to both my ghosts.

I made it to the county road by dawn
and hitched a ride on an old dairy truck.
"What happened to your shoes?" the driver said.
"No, better yet, don't tell me. Just get in."

I climbed in, and one road led to another.
And now I'm in your bar. That's probably not
the story you expected from a monk,
delivering brandy from the monastery.
Not all of us began as altar boys.

I've been there fifteen years. I like the drill—
Poverty, Chastity, and Growing Grapes.
The archbishop calls my port a miracle.
Don't tell His Grace, but I still doubt there is
an afterlife. That's not why I stay there.
This is the life I didn't want to waste.

THE BALLAD OF JESÚS ORTIZ

Jake's family were vaqueros.
They worked the cattle drives
Down from Montana to market.
They did what it took to survive.

Jake's real name was Jesús,
Which the Anglos found hard to take,
So after a couple of days,
The cowboys called him Jake.

When Jake was twelve, his father
Brought him along to ride.
"Don't waste your youth in the pueblo.
Earn by your father's side."

The days were hot and toilsome,
But all of the crew got fed.
It wasn't hard to sleep on the ground
When you've never had a bed.

Three thousand head of cattle
Grazing the prairie grass,
Three thousand head of cattle
Pushed through each mountain pass.

Three thousand head of cattle
Fording the muddy streams,
And then three thousand phantoms
Bellowing in your dreams.

At night when the coyotes called,
Jake would sometimes weep
Recalling how his mother
Sang her children to sleep.

But when he rose in the morning,
The desert air was sweet.
No sitting in a mission school
With bare and dusty feet.

And when the drive was over,
He got his pay—and then
He came back to the pueblo
Where he was one of the men.

Ten years on the open range
He led the vaquero's life,
Far from his home in Sonora,
No children and no wife.

Then Jake headed north to Wyoming
To find his winter keep
Among the Basques and Anglos
Who raised and slaughtered sheep.

He came to cold Lost Cabin
Where the Rattlesnake Mountains rise
Over the empty foothills,
Under the rainless skies.

The herders lived in dugouts
Or shacks of pine and tar.
The town had seven buildings.
The biggest was the bar.

John Okie owned the town,
The Sheep King of Wyoming.
He owned the herds. He owned the land
And every wild thing roaming.

He hired Jake for his tavern.
He let him sleep in the kitchen.
Mexicans worked hard
And didn't waste time bitching.

Tending bar was easier
Than tending cattle drives.
Jake poured the drinks while the men
Complained about their lives.

Jake never asked them questions.
He knew what he needed to know—
Men working in Lost Cabin
Had nowhere else to go.

Jake married a sheepherder's daughter,
Half Indian, half white.
They had two sons, and finally
Things in his life were right.

He told his boys his adventures
As a cowboy riding the plain.
"Papa," they cried, "will you take us
When you ride out again?"

One night he had an argument
With a herder named Bill Howard,
A deserter from the Border War,
A drunkard, and a coward.

"Bring over that bottle of whisky!
If you don't grab it, I will."
"Okie said to cut you off
Until you paid your bill."

Bill Howard slammed his fist down,
"Is this some goddamn joke,
A piss-poor Mexican peon
Telling me I'm broke?"

A little after midnight
Bill came back through the door.
Three times he shot his rifle,
And Jake fell to the floor.

Then Bill beheld his triumph
As the smoke cleared from the air—
A mirror blown into splinters,
And blood splattered everywhere.

A sudden brutal outburst
No motive could explain:
One poor man killing another
Without glory, without gain.

The tales of Western heroes
Show duels in the noonday sun,
But darkness and deception
Is how most killing is done.

Father Keller came from Lander
To lay Jake in the ground.
A posse searched the mountains
Until Bill Howard was found.

There were two more graves in Wyoming
When the clover bloomed in spring.
Two strangers drifted into town
And filled the openings.

And two tall boys departed
For the cattle drives that May
With hardly a word to their mother
Who watched them ride away.

Paul Lake (1951–2022)

Born in Baltimore, Maryland, Paul Lake published two poetry chapbooks and three full-length collections, culminating in *The Republic of Virtue* (University of Evansville Press, 2013), winner of the Richard Wilbur Poetry Award. He also produced two satirical novels, *Cry Wolf: A Political Fable* (BenBella Books, 2008) and *Among the Immortals* (Story Line Press, 1994). In essays such as "The Shape of Poetry, "The Enchanted Loom," and "Disorderly Orders"—all available for free at the online *Contemporary Poetry Review*—Lake raids the lexicons of neuroscience, particle physics, mathematics, linguistics, and natural history, mounting a defense for formal verse structures while attacking notions of indeterminacy that have overtaken Western literary criticism. He was a poetry editor for *First Things*, a journal of religion and public philosophy.

The following two entries are from Lake's 1999 collection, *Walking Backward* (Story Line Press). Publication of his debut volume, *Another Kind of Travel* (University of Chicago Press, 1988), coincided with his receipt of the Porter Fund Literary Prize, awarded annually to Arkansas writers. Since 1981, Lake had been an English professor at Arkansas Tech University. Previously, he acquired a master's degree in English and creative writing from Stanford University, where he earned a Wallace Stegner Fellowship in poetry.

INSPECTORS

He said it smiling, one hand on the open door
To let the cold air quicken the invitation,
"You want to try your luck again at checkers?"
Then entered the trailer, his boots caked thick with mud.

I didn't mind—the floor was already pebbled
With clods from my own boots, left beside the door.
I skated on the gritty linoleum,
Fetching the extra chair. Then we cleared a space
On the report-and-map-littered work table
To start a game.

"They're going to suffocate you
In this sardine can without a proper heater.
Make these cheap bastards hook you up a furnace
Or shut them down. Tell them you'll shut them down."

As usual, I lost the opening games,
But in the third kept my back row intact
And had him down two checkers. Hope made my heart
Quicken, so to fill the intervals
Between my moves, he cranked out conversation
About botched jobs and crooked contractors,
Leaning forward on one elbow above the board.

A half-made smile creased his face above his beard.
"I can *smell* a crook. Twenty years ago I learned
To sniff a bastard out—" he touched his nose
For emphasis, still smiling cagily—
"Now all I have to do is sniff the air,"
Then he chuckled as if enjoying a private joke.

"The Bataan Death March—you ever heard of that?
That's where I went to school to study bastards—
You learned quick there which ones would sell you out.
After our march across that sweat-box island,
The Japs shipped us back home, like souvenirs.
That's what we were to them—living property.
It wasn't work they wanted out of us,
Though they kept up the pretense. How much work
Can men starved down to skeletons perform?
They got their satisfaction watching men
Once enemies brought down to animal level,
Then lower than animals, turning on each other.
After three years there I weighed eighty-seven pounds.
Sometimes I got so desperate with hunger,
I'd save dried kernels from their horses' shit
Until I'd filled a can, boil it, and eat.
Once in the saving mood, I rat-holed quinine
They gave us for malaria. When I had enough—
What I *thought* was enough—I swallowed it all,
But it only made me sick enough to wish
Some other skeleton would finish me,
Though no one had the heart to do the job.

"Three years of that. They finally made me foreman
Of a work gang, with three women under me—
Jap women. One, I planned on marrying
After the war, but after liberation
A first lieutenant took me in his office
And told me what a mistake I'd almost made."

He paused to study the board in thoughtful silence,
Then squinted, adding,

"If I were back there now
And had to trust my life to other men,

Which one of us inspectors do you think
I'd trust my life with—try and guess his name."

I thought a minute, calling up names and faces.
"I'm not sure . . . maybe Duffy, Duffy Landers."

"That sneaky son-of-a-bitch?
                                        No, guess again."

I tried another name. He seemed amused
Or scornful as I ticked off half a dozen,
So I tried to think what grim criteria
A survivor of a death-camp might employ—
What fatal tic or slant-wise look of the eyes
Might give the telltale sign of a fink or traitor.
Looked at that way, we all seemed half-suspicious.
I wondered how I rated on the scale
He used to measure men, then gave up guessing.
"So what did you do when you got back to the States?"

His eyes wrinkled at the corners.
                                        "Stayed in the
    army.
And here's a funny thing that happened there
When I'd been home a while. This crazy buddy
Told me how we could supplement our pay
By playing guinea pigs at Edgewood Arsenal—
They had some kind of gas they had to test.
I thought, Why not—what could they do to me
I hadn't had done ten times worse already,
So we both signed up. I found out I was wrong.

"They locked us in a room with one glass wall,
Strapped on our masks, and then sat down to watch.

My buddy passed out first—the gas had leaked
Right through the mechanism—I woke up later
In the hospital, stiff as a wooden plank,
And for six months I couldn't twitch a muscle.
My buddy had it worse. He was paralyzed
For the best part of a year. But the worst news was
That after we could walk, we still weren't men
Entirely: Our peckers wouldn't stiffen.
They said it was a normal side-effect
Of nerve gas, but my buddy took it hard
And swore he'd marry the first girl with the touch
To make his flagpole stand up to the breeze.

I never saw a man so full of himself
The next year when I showed up at his wedding.
Now he's a colonel. I guess that goes to show
The kind of pricks they take for officers.

"So make your move ...
                                        You've made it close this
    time.
I'll give you that.
                                You ever figure out
Which one of us inspectors that I'd trust
With the only life I'll ever have to live?
You're looking at him—that's the truth of it.
What say we have another go-around
After I pull this game out of the fire?
I'll put my boots on while you study it."

I moved a piece, then pushed my chair away
As things grew clear.

                                        "Is that your move?" Now smiling,
He rubbed his palms together. "Go on, king me."

WALKING BACKWARD

You're wondering why I'm back in Minnesota—
I know it wasn't business that brought you here.
What business could ever get you to Bemidji
With its one gallery filled with Indian art?
Pots, blankets, beads . . . hardly your cup of tea.
You've come to put me on the straight and narrow
Runway back to Minneapolis.
New York, or Boston—anyplace but here—
And think that while you're doing me a favor
You'll do yourself one, too, but I won't go.
After so much trouble, mastering the trick
Of walking backward. I can't turn around
As easily as that. I've come too far.
Instead, I'll tell you of a man I met
That might help me explain what brought me back
To my hometown against all sense and reason
After twenty years.

The fellow's name's Sam Harper.
I met him on the shoulder of the highway
Beyond the mall my first week back in town—
I passed him walking north as I drove south.
I *thought* that it was north. When I got closer,
I saw that he was walking in reverse,
Heel-first, in my direction down the highway,
Arms swinging at his sides so casually,
You'd think he thought that way was natural.
It was—*is*, I should say—at least for him.
Of course he once walked like the rest of us,
But took it on himself to make the change.
That's what he wanted when he started out—

To make a change. I spoke to him about it
One afternoon when he turned down our street.
It was unsettling the way he talked—
Him backing up, me walking straight at him
So that we kept a steady space between us.
I had the chance to study him up close.
He wore a string of sleigh bells round his shoulders
Which jingled with each step, and in one hand
Held a black plastic garbage bag, half full.
He told me that the sleigh bells were to warn
Pedestrians of his sudden blind approach;
The plastic sack he used or pick up litter,
Undoing others' damage where he passed.
It took more nerve to ask the obvious
Question about his walking, so I spoke
Quickly before it had the chance to misfire.
I'm glad I did. He never hesitated,
But softly, without shame or condescension,
Explained it with a biblical directness.
He said his life had gone so poorly forward,
He'd try the other way now for a change.
Though he kept his past a bit mysterious—
He'd done some time . . . he didn't say for what—
I doubt he'd ever maimed or killed someone.
If there'd been sins and wreckage in his life,
They didn't seem so radical in nature
As to make him turn his life around like that
In such literal fashion.

                    My next door neighbor
Explained that Sam is half Objibwe Indian
And half Norwegian, as if that might account
For the odd nature of his turnaround.

He didn't say which half gave the idea.
The truth is, no tradition Sam could hear of,
New World or Old, would urge such an odd course.
It came half-breed like him: He got it watching
That Dustin Hoffman movie, *Little Big Man*,
In which an Indian in a minor role
Walked, ran—even rode a horse—while backing up.
And yet, despite the comic origin
Of his self-imposed penance, Sam makes it seem
Right somehow. In another age we might
Have called it holiness and Sam a saint—
Now we dismiss it simply as eccentric.

That's how my own change came: Watching television.
One night I absent-mindedly turned it on
And found myself in 1968
Vietnam. Automatic rifle fire
Echoed in stereo around my room,
Raking the rubber fronds of jungle trees
As the sound-track rocked with recoils, trumpets, shouts,
And a thatch-roofed village blossomed into fire.
Back then, of course, the actors weren't so handsome,
The pictures weren't so steady or so clear.
This was the dream of some vice president
Of network scheduling set in its slot
Of family viewing time to serve up action
In healthy dollops along with aspirin,
Tampons and deodorants. . . .

I turned the set off,
Then sat in silence for an hour or two,
Remembering how close I came to being
An actor in that scene—though, naturally,
Like all my friends—like all of both our friends—

Not only did I beat the draft myself,
I never knew a single man who didn't.
Those whose deferments were reviewed or lost
Still always somehow landed on their feet:
A friendly doctor said they were unstable—
I know an atheist who got deferred
On conscientious grounds, though he's no Quaker—
While others simply got a lucky draw
In the lottery or fled to Canada.
You won't believe how I avoided service.
I flunked my physical in perfect health.
By concentrating, I could raise my blood pressure
By thirty, forty points—I don't know how.
It's funny, isn't it? Then I felt clever,
And I suppose it was good luck, at that—
I didn't have to leave my native country,
Spend years in jail, or match my wits against
The skepticism of those staunch Lutherans
On my draft board in wild hopes of a C.O.
Instead, I got back on the Trailways bus
They brought us in on and went back to college
To learn to paint. They drafted someone else.
That's what I thought of that night as I watched
The blank-faced television—of that someone
Who went instead of me, that nameless other
Too dumb or forthright to resist, that boy
From my hometown or near it whom my draft board
Called up its insatiable hunger
In my place and sent off to that foul war.

If I had done things differently—stood up
And borne the consequences at some cost
To peace of mind and body, I'd feel better—
Different, at least—though I'm not so naïve

As to believe the wheels of that machine
Which gobbled up and crushed all those young bodies
Would boggle up its cogs on my account.
No wonder we keep turning back to it
In memory and television screenplays:
We want to give those times another ending,
To crown our acts with glory, find heroism
Where only the grim will to live survived.
Instead, we ought to put on bells and walk
Backward to collect the waste we've laid
As the frontiers of our monstrous egotism
Expanded. To contract our destiny
To the borders of some known and well-loved place
We might defend with courage, justice, honor.
I like to think that Sam might make it back
With all his walking, clearing us a path
Across an unlittered North America,
Where we might go, made festive by our sleigh bells,
Growing year by year more joyous with thanksgivings.

Rita Dove (b. 1952)

Rita Dove's most renowned narrative efforts are *Sonata Mulattica: A Life in Five Movements and a Short Play* (W. W. Norton, 2009) and her Pulitzer Prize-winning *Thomas and Beulah* (Carnegie-Mellon University Press, 1986), a semifictional sequence of forty-four free-verse poems based on the lives of Dove's maternal grandparents. The narrative impulse also guides her "Cameos" sequence from an earlier volume, *On the Bus with Rosa Parks* (W. W. Norton, 1999). "The Bistro Styx" is taken from Dove's 1995 collection, *Mother Love* (W. W. Norton, 1995), which explores mother-daughter relations by retelling the Greek myth of Demeter and Persephone. In this inviting poem, wry observation is a hallmark.

Born in Akron, Ohio, and educated at Miami University, Tübingen University (Germany), and the University of Iowa, Dove teaches creative writing at the University of Virginia. She is, with Bob Dylan, the most decorated contributor to this anthology. In 2022–23 alone, she won an honorary National Book Award, the Rebekah Johnson Bobbitt National Prize for Poetry from the Library of Congress, and the Ruth Lilly Poetry Prize from the Poetry Foundation. Earlier, she had picked up a Gold Medal for Poetry from the American Academy of Arts and Letters, the Wallace Stevens Award from the American Academy of American Poets, lifetime achievement awards from the Fulbright Association and the Library of Virginia, the National Humanities Medal and the National Medal of Arts from two different presidents, and—even if we overlook twenty-nine honorary doctorates and a laureateship at the Library of Congress—several other trophies for her life's work. Her most recent book of poems is *Playlist for the Apocalypse* (W. W. Norton, 2021).

THE BISTRO STYX

She was thinner, with a mannered gauntness
as she paused just inside the double
glass doors to survey the room, silvery cape
billowing dramatically behind her. *What's this*,

I thought, lifting a hand until
she nodded and started across the parquet;
that's when I saw she was dressed all in gray,
from a kittenish cashmere skirt and cowl

down to the graphite signature of her shoes.
"Sorry I'm late," she panted, though
she wasn't, sliding into the chair, her cape

tossed off in a shudder of brushed steel.
We kissed. Then I leaned back to peruse
my blighted child, this wary aristocratic mole.

"How's business?" I asked, and hazarded
a motherly smile to keep from crying out:
Are you content to conduct your life
as a cliché and, what's worse,

an anachronism, the brooding artist's demimonde?
Near the rue Princesse they had opened
a gallery *cum* souvenir shop which featured
fuzzy off-color Monets next to his acrylics, no doubt,

plus beared African drums and the occasional miniature
gargoyle from Notre Dame the Great Artist had
carved at breakfast with a pocket knife.

"Tourists love us. The Parisians, of course"—
she blushed—"are amused, though not without
a certain admiration . . ."
The Chateaubriand

arrived on a bone-white plate, smug and absolute
in its fragrant crust, a black plug steaming
like the heart plucked from the chest of a worthy enemy;
one touch with her fork sent pink juices streaming.

"Admiration for what?" Wine, a bloody
Pinot Noir, brought color to her cheeks. "Why,
the aplomb with which we've managed
to support our Art"—meaning he'd convinced

her to pose nude for his appalling canvases,
faintly futuristic landscapes strewn
with carwrecks and bodies being chewed

by rabid cocker spaniels. "I'd like to come by
the studio," I ventured, "and see the new stuff."
"Yes, if you wish . . ." A delicate rebuff

before the warning: "He dresses all
in black now. Me, he drapes in blues and carmine—
and even though I think it's kinda cute,
in company I tend toward more muted shades."

She paused and had the grace
to drop her eyes. She did look ravishing,
spookily insubstantial, a lipstick ghost on tissue,
or as if one stood on a fifth-floor terrace

peering through a fringe of rain at Paris'
dreaming chimney pots, each sooty issue
wobbling skyward in an ecstatic oracular spiral.

"And he never thinks of food. I wish
I didn't have to plead with him to eat. . . ." Fruit
and cheese appeared, arrayed on leaf-green dishes.

I stuck with café crème. "This Camembert's
so ripe," she joked, "it's practically grown hair,"
mucking a golden glob complete with parsley sprig
onto a heel of bread. Nothing seemed to fill

her up: She swallowed, sliced into a pear,
speared each tear-shaped lavaliere
and popped the dripping mess into her pretty mouth.
Nowhere the bright tufted fields, weighted

vines and sun poured down out of the south.
"But are you happy?" Fearing, I whispered it
quickly. "What? You know, Mother"—

she bit into the starry rose of a fig—
"one really should try the fruit here."
I've lost her, I thought, and called for the bill.

Alberto Rios (b. 1952)

In an essay, "Magical Realism and the Sociology of Possibility" (*Poetry Northwest*, Winter and Spring 2020), Alberto Rios reminds us that one antecedent for the term "magical realism," as it is currently used to denote a subgenre of fiction, is "the Spanish phrase *lo real maravilloso*," which "translates more literally as the marvelous real or marvelous reality." Crediting the Cuban novelist Alejo Carpentier (1904–80) with coining the expression in 1949, Rios resists a sense of frivolity lurking in the more common English equivalent. Magical realism, for him, is about the recombinant possibilities of language and culture in evoking a profoundly intimate human experience. He writes: "The stakes are high because, in a word, we do not believe other ways of living. Reality is our reality, whoever we are."

The three narratives here have an affinity with magical realism as practiced by many of Latin America's best-known novelists and poets. "True Story of the Pins" comes from Rios's 1982 collection, *Whispering to Fool the Wind* (Sheep Meadow Press), which Donald Justice (1925–2004) chose for the Walt Whitman Award. Born in Nogales, Arizona, Rios obtained a bachelor's degree and an MFA from the University of Arizona. For more than thirty-five years, he has taught at Arizona State University, where he is a regents' professor and directs the Virginia G. Piper Center for Creative Writing. In 2013, he became the state's inaugural poet laureate.

Capirotada (University of New Mexico Press, 1999), a memoir, tells the story of Rios's childhood in Nogales. Among other notable volumes are *The Smallest Muscle in the Human Body* (Copper Canyon Press, 2002), a finalist for the National Book Award, and *The Theater of Night* (Copper Canyon Press, 2005), which won the PEN/Open Book Award (formerly the Beyond the Margins Award). He has published three collections of short stories and, in 2020, *A Map of All Good Things: A Picaresque Novel* (University of Arizona Press). In the same year, Copper Canyon Press brought out his most recent poetry volume, *Not Go Away Is My Name*.

TRUE STORY OF THE PINS

Pins are always plentiful
but one day they were not
and your Uncle Humberto
who collected all the butterflies
you see here on the walls,
was crazy looking for some
and he went to your cousin
Graciela the hard seamstress
who has pins it is rumored
even in hard times
but when she found out
why he wanted them
because the wind from the south
who was her friend
since the days of her
childhood on the sea
told her, she firmly refused
your poor Uncle Humberto
whose picture is here
on the wall behind you,
did you feel his eyes,
and he went into the most terrible
of rages, too terrible
for a butterfly collector
we all said afterward
and he burst the vein
that grew like a great snake
on his small forehead
and he died on the dirt
floor of Graciela's house

who of course felt sick
and immediately went
and put pins, this is what has
made her hard, through
the bright wings of the butterflies
Humberto had prepared
since he was after all
her father and she
could afford no better
light of perpetuity.

FIRST WORDS

By itself the piano was playing a waltz.
The old couple had been left just then with an orphan
And they told him, *this is a wooden cricket.*
The boy called out at once, far too loudly he knew,
It's not the way things used to be.
People were happy with plain crickets.
He had never seen anything quite so alone.
They asked, w*hat are you crying for, small boy?*
To them he knew he had to answer.
I should have controlled myself, of course.
The future of myself depends on it.
But the cricket's voice he thought was like the forest,
And each of the notes played from that paper list were people
Who had lost their nations, and consequently their health.
I've had a knack for book-learning, he said.
And that's how I know about things.
They looked at him and saw it was true.
How long have you had your infirmity, and
Were you born so? He nodded his head to say yes.
They were he could tell both embarrassed,
Able only to drop into the single words of children.
The man of the couple came over to apologize
For all the things that had ever been wrong,
And quietly the boy nodded again, yes,
Hugging carefully the man's crooked back.

REFUGIO'S HAIR

In the old days of our family,
My grandmother was a young woman
Whose hair was as long as the river.
She lived with her sisters on the ranch
La Calera—The Land of the Lime—
And her days were happy.

But her uncle Carlos lived there too,
Carlos whose soul had the edge of a knife.
One day, to teach her to ride a horse,
He made her climb on the fastest one,
Bareback, and sit there
As he held its long face in his arms.

And then he did the unspeakable deed
For which he would always be remembered:
He called for the handsome baby Pirrin
And he placed the child in her arms.
With that picture of a Madonna on horseback
He slapped the shank of the horse's rear leg.

The horse did what a horse must,
Racing full toward the bright horizon.
But first he ran under the *álamo* trees
To rid his back of this unfair weight:
This woman full of tears
And this baby full of love.

When they reached the trees and went under,
Her hair, which had trailed her,
Equal in its magnificence to the tail of the horse,

That hair rose up and flew into the branches
As if it were a thousand arms,
All of them trying to save her.

The horse ran off and left her,
The baby still in her arms,
The two of them hanging from her hair.
The baby looked only at her
And did not cry, so steady was her cradle.
Her sisters came running to save them.

But the hair would not let go.
From its fear it held on and had to be cut,
All of it, from her head.
From that day on, my grandmother
Wore her hair short like a scream,
But it was long like a river in her sleep.

Gjertrud Schnackenberg (b. 1953)

Gjertrud Schnackenberg's poetic gifts announced themselves early. While attending Mount Holyoke College, she twice entered and twice won the Glascock Intercollegiate Poetry Contest, the nation's oldest competition for undergraduate poetry. Between her first and second books—*Portraits and Elegies* (D. R. Godine, 1982) and *The Lamplit Answer* (Farrar, Straus & Giroux, 1985)—she bagged the Rome Prize from the American Academy of Arts and Letters and was chosen by the poet and classicist Robert Fitzgerald for the Lavan Younger Poets Award from the American Academy of Poets.

Born in Takoma, Washington, and now living in Boston, Schnackenberg has been honored with fellowships or visiting scholar roles from the National Endowment for the Arts, the Guggenheim Foundation, the Radcliffe Institute for Advanced Study at Harvard University, Oxford University (St. Catherine's College), and the Getty Research Institute. In 2004, she received the Berlin Prize from the American Academy in Berlin.

In terms of books, Schnackenberg's output has been slender but mighty. *A Gilded Lapse of Time* (Farrar, Straus & Giroux, 1992) pays tribute to Dante and Osip Mandelstam and extends her dominion of religious and historical subjects in poetry. *The Throne of Labdacus* (Farrar, Straus & Giroux, 2000) retells the myth of Oedipus and other Greek stories. Her next collection, *Heavenly Questions* (Farrar, Straus & Giroux, 2010), links six long poems in an elegy provoked by the 2002 death of her husband, the philosopher Robert Nozick. For this book, she earned the Griffin Poetry Prize. In 2024, Arrowsmith published Schnackenberg's *St. Matthew Passion*, poems honoring Bach's sacred oratorio, after which the volume is named.

TWO TALES OF CLUMSY

1

When Clumsy harks the gladsome ting-a-lings
Of dinner chimes that Mrs. Clumsy rings,
His two hands winglike at his most bald head,
Then Clumsy readies Clumsy to be fed.
He pulls from satchel huge a tiny chair,
And waggling his pillowed derriere

He hitches up his pants to gently sit.
Like two ecstatic doves his white hands flit
Tucking his bib in quickly, then, all thumbs,
They brush away imaginary crumbs
From knee-high table with dismissive air.
With fists wrapped round his giant silverware

He shuts his eyes and puckers up for kisses.
In such a pose Clumsy awaits his Mrs.,
Rubbing his hungry ribs. But oh, alack,
Quite unbeknownst to Clumsy, at his back
The circle of a second spotlight shows
That No-No has delivered fatal blows

To Mrs. Clumsy since that happy time
She summoned Clumsy with her dinner chime.
And there is Clumsy's darling lying dead.
How like a rubber ball bounces her head
As No-No drags her feet-first from this life.
Then No-No dresses up as Clumsy's wife,

Her scarf now silhouettes his long hooked nose,
His long bones rattle in her frilly clothes

As No-No bears a tray of cups and plates
Into the light where puckered Clumsy waits.
Hearing her footstep soft makes Clumsy take
The pucker from his lips and sweetly break

Into falsetto greetings, then resume
His lisps into a kiss. But this is doom,
And hideously silent No-No stands.
When Clumsy parts his eyelids both his hands
Fly up as if on strings and Clumsy screams.
The tears squirt from his ducts a dozen streams,

His mouth blubbers, inelegantly smeared,
"Where is she, No-No? Oh, I am afeared!"
Then No-No lifts up Clumsy's trembly chin,
And leans to hiss with loud stage whisper in
The big pink ear of Clumsy. "My dear friend,"
No-No enunciates, "this is The End."

2

Disguised as Doctor of Philosophy
In academic haberdashery
By dint of hood and black capacious gown,
No-No wipes off the blackboard up and down,
His black sleeve floating outward with each lunge,
The black streaks glisten from his dampened sponge,

While Clumsy sharpens pencils two feet long
To little stubs and wets them with his tongue,
Then smooths his pad of paper with gloved fists.
He lifts his sleeves a fraction at the wrists
And twirls his hands around like windmill sails
To soothe his nerves, then drums his muffled nails

Until the Doctor claps his hands rat-tat
And picks his pointer up and points it at
His eager pupil with the jumbo ears:
"Compose a paragraph." And Clumsy clears
His throat a dozen times to soft aver,
"I don't know how to write with letters sir."

At which the Doctor hides with sleeve a smile
Most uncontrollable and fraught with guile,
Until, authority regained, he says,
"In that case you may dictate sentences
Which you most which to write, and I'll record
Your words for you to copy from the board."

Now Clumsy tries to think of what to write.
He cranes his neck around stage-left and -right,
He gazes toward the rafters thinking hard
And sometimes shakes his head as to discard
Ideas he finds less than adequate,
Then caroling a joyous "I know what!"

He pulls a giant light-bulb from a sack
And holds it overhead and puts it back,
And in his vast excitement both his hands
Pull up his earlobe-anchored rubber bands
To lift from scalp his tiny frizzy wig:
"I'd like to start with 'God is very big.'"

Erupting laughter nearly knocks quite down
The Doctor in his nearly empty gown,
He whirls on heel and cuts his hooting off:
"My theologian! Fellow *philosophe*!
Your disquisition bears the resonance
Of truth's unique, unutterable sense

But yet, being pedantic and antique,
This mind of mine must tinker, weigh, and seek,
And wonder if together you and I
For sake of scholarship should specify
How big God is?" Thus groping for the truth
About the size of God makes pink smoke poof

From Clumsy's ears in jets, and fire alarms
Go off backstage as, lowered head on arms,
Full sixty seconds Clumsy cogitates.
The Doctor snaps his chalk in two and waits.
Clumsy looks up and No-No utters "Yes?"
"Bigger than cloud formations, I would guess."

"Bigger than clouds! Dear fellow! I should say
I never would have thought of God that way!
Then let's begin." And No-No sets the chalk
Tick-ticking on the board like time-bomb clock
While Clumsy wraps his pencil finger-wise
And sets it on the page and squints his eyes

At No-No's blackboard words so white and clean
And neat and straight with spaces in between,
And then, his page two inches from his nose,
He copies out in crooked uphill rows:
"I, Clumsy, hereby give and wittingly
My soul to No-No for Eternity."

DARWIN IN 1881

Sleepless as Prospero back in his bedroom
In Milan, with all his miracles
Reduced to sailors' tales,
He sits up in the dark. The islands loom.
His seasickness upwells,
Silence creeps by in memory as it crept
By him on water, while the sailors slept,
From broken eggs and vacant tortoise shells.
His voyage around the cape of middle age
Comes, with a feat of insight, to a close,
The same way Prospero's
Ended before he left the stage
To be led home across the blue-white sea,
When he had spoken of the clouds and globe,
Breaking his wand, and taking off his robe:
Knowledge increases unreality.

He quickly dresses.
Form wavers like his shadow on the stair
As he descends, in need of air
To cure his dizziness,
Down past the ship-sunk emptiness
Of grownup children's rooms and hallways where
The family portraits stare,
All haunted by each other's likenesses.

Outside, the orchard and a piece of moon
Are islands, he an island as he walks,
Brushing against weed stalks.
By hook and plume
The seeds gathering on his trouser legs

Are archipelagoes, like nests he sees
Shadowed in branching, ramifying trees,
Each with unique expressions in its eggs.
Different islands conjure
Different beings; different beings call
From different isles. And after all
His scrutiny of Nature
All he can see
Is how it will grow small, fade, disappear,
A coastline fading from a traveler
Aboard a survey ship. Slowly,
As coasts depart,
Nature had left behind a naturalist
Bound for a place where species don't exist,
Where no emergence has a counterpart.

He's heard from friends
About the other night, the banquet hall
Ringing with bravos—like a curtain call,
He thinks, when the performance ends,
Failing to summon from the wings
An actor who had lost his taste for verse,
Having beheld, in larger theaters,
Much greater banquet vanishings
Without the quaint device and thunderclap
Required in Act 3.
He wrote, Let your indulgence set me free,

To the Academy, and took a nap
Beneath a *London Daily* tent,
Then puttered on his hothouse walk
Watching his orchids beautifully stalk
Their unreturning paths, where each descendant
Is the last—

Their inner staircases
Haunted by vanished insect faces
So tiny, so intolerably vast.
And, while they gave his proxy the award,
He dined in Downe and stayed up rather late
For backgammon with his beloved mate,
Who reads his books and is, quite frankly, bored.

Now, done with beetle jaws and beaks of gulls
And bivalve hinges, now, utterly done,
One miracle remains, and only one.
An ocean swell of sickness rushes, pulls,
He leans against the fence
And lights a cigarette and deeply draws,
Done with fixed laws,
Done with experiments
Within his greenhouse heaven where
His offspring, Frank, for half the afternoon
Played, like an awkward angel, his bassoon
Into the humid air
So he could tell
If sound would make a Venus's-flytrap lose.
And, done for good with scientific prose,
That raging hell
Of tortured grammars writhing on their stakes,

He'd turned to his memoirs, chuckling to write
About his boyhood in an upright
Home: a boy preferring gartersnakes
To schoolwork, a lazy, strutting liar
Who quite provoked her aggravated look,
Shushed in the drawing room behind her book,
His bossy sister itching with desire

To tattletale—yes, that was good.
But even then, much like the conjurer
Grown cranky with impatience to abjure
All his gigantic works and livelihood
In order to immerse
Himself in tales where he could be the man
In Once upon a time there was a man,

He'd quite by chance beheld the universe:
A disregarded game of chess
Between two love-dazed heirs
Who fiddle with the tiny pairs
Of statues in their hands, while numberless
Abstract unseen
Combinings on the silent board remain
Unplayed forever when they leave the game
To turn, themselves, into a king and queen.
Now, like the coming day,
Inhaled smoke illuminates his nerves.
He turns, taking the sandwalk as it curves
Back to the yard, the house, the entrance way
Where, not to waken her,

He softly shuts the door,
And leans against it for a spell before
He climbs the stairs, holding the banister,
Up to their room: there
Emma sleeps, moored
In illusion, blown past the storm he conjured
With his book, into a harbor
Where it all comes clear,
Where island beings leap from shape to shape
As to escape

Their terrifying turns to disappear.
He lies down on the quilt,
He lies down like a fabulous-headed
Fossil in a vanished riverbed,
In ocean drifts, in canyon floors, in silt,
In lime, in deepening blue ice,
In cliffs obscured as clouds gather and float;
He lies down in his boots and overcoat,
And shuts his eyes.

Mary Jo Salter (b. 1954)

"Frost at Midnight" originally appeared in Mary Jo Salter's 1994 collection *Sunday Skaters*, a nominee for the National Book Critics Circle Award. The poem carries an epigraph from Samuel Taylor Coleridge's blank verse meditation of the same title. Although Salter's subject, Robert Frost, remains America's premier storyteller in blank verse, she uses the form to more panoramic effect here, zooming in and out with her lens, and covering multiple time points. Readers may wish to consult a poem of a similar name: Robert Lowell's "Robert Frost at Midnight." An unrhymed sonnet, it too has roots in the turmoil of Frost's family biography.

Born in Grand Rapids, Michigan, Salter grew up also in Detroit and Baltimore and earned bachelor's and master's degrees from Harvard University and the University of Cambridge, respectively. At Harvard, she studied with Elizabeth Bishop. Salter taught for twenty-three years at Mount Holyoke College and then became Krieger-Eisenhower Professor in the Writing Seminars at Johns Hopkins University (2007–2022), where she is now a professor emerita.

Henry Purcell in Japan (Knopf, 1985) marked Salter's poetic debut. Its successor, *Unfinished Painting* (Knopf, 1989), won the Lamont Poetry Prize (now the James Laughlin Award) for the year's best second collection by any poet. *Open Shutters* (Knopf, 2003) was a *New York Times* Notable Book of the Year. Her most recent poetry book is *Zoom Rooms* (Knopf, 2022), whose title poem is a sonnet sequence. Among other volumes are *The Surveyors* (Knopf, 2017), *It's Hard to Say: Selected Poems* (Waywiser Press, 2015), *Nothing by Design* (Knopf, 2013), and *A Phone Call to the Future* (Knopf, 2008)—another selection of previous poems. She has additionally authored a children's book, *The Moon Comes Home* (Knopf, 1989) , and a play, *Falling Bodies*, which premiered in 2004. A former assistant poetry editor for *The Atlantic* and staff editor for *The New Republic*, she coedited the fourth, fifth, and sixth editions of the *Norton Anthology of Poetry*. In 2024, she guest-edited Scribner's *The Best American Poetry* collection for that year.

FROST AT MIDNIGHT

> For I was reared
> In the great city, pent 'mid cloisters dim,
> And saw nought lovely but the sky and stars.
> But *thou*, my babe! shalt wander like a breeze
> By lakes and sandy shores . . .
>
> —*Coleridge*

1.

His children tuckered out, tucked in (three girls
jammed in one bedroom, the boy in the only other),
and Elinor dozing where the dining room
would be if they'd had room, the "Yank from Yankville,"
as he liked to call himself, was wide awake.
It was midnight, on the fifteenth of September,
1912, and Frost was thirty-eight.
Tonight, he'd stay up late before the fire
in his Morris chair, as he often did, and write
to Susan Hayes Ward of *The Independent*,
who'd been the first to put his name in print.
Hard to believe that he, New Hampshire teacher
and half-hearted farmer, poet of little note,
just days before had boarded *The Parisian*
from Boston to Glasgow, then taken the train to London
with all of those now sleeping in his care.
Or that a tip from a retired policeman
(they knew no one in England, not a soul)
had led them to the village of Beaconsfield,
and a cottage called The Bungalow (or Bung Hole,
in the family lingo) for a monthly rent
of twenty dollars. Why were they here?

They'd flipped a coin.
Heads England, tails Vancouver—the nickel rose
silver like the moon from the Atlantic
they'd cross, sea-sick, to see it land again.
And now they lived behind a looming hedge
of American laurel, taller than any he
had seen at home. He wasn't here to pose
at Englishness, although the place was quaint,
all right: the muffin man had stepped
out of the nursery rhyme to walk their street
with the flypaper man; the knife-grinder; the man
who dangled pots and pans for sale from a wagon
drawn by a donkey. All this the children loved,
and Elinor might still fulfill her dream
sometime of sleeping under thatch. But no,
he hadn't come to write about such things.
At the bottom of his trunk the manuscripts
of some hundred poems waited to be sorted
into two books or three, and he'd write more
about the world he knew and had left behind.

His firstborn Elliott dead (his fault, he thought—
he'd called for the wrong doctor); later a daughter,
her mother's namesake, who lived not quite two days—
he wouldn't stop to brood on those troubles now.
Tonight his mood was defiant, even "aberrant,"
he wrote to Susan Ward. He'd "achieve something
solid enough to sandbag editors with."
After all, it was just a few miles from here
that Milton, in a cottage like this (shared
with *his* three daughters) finished *Paradise Lost*.
And a mile or two the other way that Gray,
redeemed by glory, lay in a country churchyard.

"To London town what is it but a run?"
he closed in singsong, adding he'd step out
to the yard, before bed, to watch the city lights
in the distance "flaring like a dreary dawn."
Not quite—but a visionary flourish?
A biographer named Walsh, who went to live
in The Bungalow long after, noted how
London remains some twenty-one miles off.
Equipped with a naked eye, then, Frost could never
have caught the faintest glimmer of the city.
But was this the night the first biographer
would write of as the turning point? The night
the poems were taken from the trunk and sorted
into the first of all the selves he left?
It was sometime in September or October.
Frost sat on the cold floor. From time to time,
he'd crumple a ball and toss it in the fire.
He saw, in the hearth, the lights of London blaze
each time he found a poem to sacrifice:
that way the ones he saved could shine the brighter.
Or it may be, as the curling pages turned
brilliant a fierce instant, then to ash,
he was thinking of the sallow leaves that fell
indifferently outside, beyond the laurel,
and was terrified of their unwritten message.
By October's end, the book was done and out,
typed by his eldest, Lesley; a Mrs. Nutt
(who shrugged "the day of poetry is past")
allowed she was nonetheless "disposed" to publish.
A Boy's Will. He'd left boyhood after all.

2.

As a boy might skip a stone across a pond,
skim over fifty-one Octobers, to
the President with the winning smile. He'd fall
in less than one month's time in the Dallas sun.
He comes to return the favor of a white-
maned legend, lionized past recognition.
Once, squinting in the glare, fumbling with pages
that seemed on fire, the poet had declaimed
by heart (though he misspoke the young man's name)
a poem to inaugurate The New Frontier.
Robert Frost is dead; a library in his honor
at Amherst College today is dedicated.
"He knew the midnight as well as the high noon,"
Kennedy says. And now the library shelves
behind him will begin to accrete their proof.
Shoulder to shoulder, books file in like soldiers
to settle the literary territory
of one who has been seen as saint and monster.

Our story goes back to Derry, New Hampshire, years
before England. Lesley was six or so.
In the middle of the night, she was awakened
by her father, who conducted her downstairs,
her feet cold on the floor. At the kitchen table
her mother wept, face hidden in her hands.
It was then that Lesley spotted the revolver.
"Take your choice," Frost said, as he waved the thing
between himself and Elinor—a less bracing
alternative than a poem unwritten yet
would give between two roads in a yellow wood.
"Before morning," he warned, "one of us will be dead."

The child was returned to bed. And only after
she'd tucked him in the earth would her memory
be brought to light—or fixed, at least, in print.
Was it true? Or a vivid, fluttering scarf of nightmare?
It wrapped, somehow, around the family neck.
For it wasn't Lesley, but her brother Carol
who—whether or not the grisly tale was real—
rewrote it with his life. It was the ninth
of October, 1940; he was thirty-eight.
He'd kept his own boy, Prescott, up for hours
with talk of his failures as a poet-farmer;
of fears (but here the doctors would be wrong—
his wife lived on for more than fifty years)
that Lillian might not even last the night.
When Prescott drifted off, he took the shotgun
he'd bought for Lillian as a wedding gift
and went downstairs, before the sun could rise,
to turn it on himself.

Strange how in families
time seeps through all we do, so that the order
in which things happen seems to bow before
the dreamlike authority of metaphor.
Marjorie, the baby, dies in childbirth;
Elinor (who was "the unspoken half,"
Frost said, "of everything I ever wrote"—
if it wasn't true, one has no doubt he meant it)
is stricken at the heart while climbing stairs,
as if away from the scenes to come, when Carol
step by step descends flights of despair,
and Irma's mind unravels in and out
of the hospital. Time spirals to rearrange
events to show us something beyond change.

"Two things are sure," Carol's father had written
to Lillian in the midst of a world war
in which, he thought, a man might best have died
a soldier. "He was driven distracted by life
and he was perfectly brave." And yet he runs
his hand across more pages, as if to smooth
the mound of a new grave: Carol's mind
was one, he writes this time, with a "twist from childhood."
Think how, the year before, he'd raced through stop-signs:
his eyes veered "off the road ahead too often."

Now Frost is eighty-eight. He can see ahead.
Poet of chance and choice, who tossed a coin
but knew which side his bread was buttered on,
who said, "The most inalienable right of man
is to go to hell in his own way," here he is
in a hospital bed, a hell he hasn't made.
He has a letter from Lesley, who knows him for
the stubborn vanities and selfless gestures.
She knows, dear girl, the words to make him well,
if anything can make him well. She calls him
"Robert Coeur de Lion." Too weak to write,
he dictates a final letter back to her.
"You're something of a Lesley de Lion
yourself," he says, and he commends the children's
poems she's been working on. It's good
to have a way with the young. The old man
hasn't lost his knack, even in prose,
for giving the truth the grandeur of a cadence.
"I'd rather be taken for brave than anything else."

David Mason (b. 1954)

David Mason, with Mark Jarman, edited *Rebel Angels: 25 Poets of the New Formalism* (Story Line Press, 1996), an anthology that shares many poets with the present one. In the preface to *Rebel Angels*, the editors drew attention to the concomitant rise of narrative and formal verse in the 1980s and 1990s. Labels such as Expansive Poetry and New Narrative have been used to describe this synthesis, and Mason is one of its leading practitioners.

His verse novel, *Ludlow* (Red Hen Press, 2010), charts the lives of Colorado immigrants who ended up as victims in the Ludlow Massacre, which occurred in 1914 when state militia attacked striking mine workers and their families. The three selections here show what Mason can do with narrative on a smaller scale. "Gusev," a pantoum, is based on the eponymous story by Anton Chekhov (1860–1904), about a soldier dying of consumption in a ship's hospital cabin.

Born in Bellingham, Washington, and a graduate of Colorado College and Rochester University, Mason lived and worked in Greece on two separate occasions. There he befriended the author Sir Patrick Leigh Fermor (1915–2011), whom he has preferred to call not a travel writer but "a poet, a fantastic re-creator of experience, a maker of paradisiacal sentences that leave me hungry for life." Beyond his collections of poetry, Mason has produced a memoir of his time in Greece (*News from the Village: Aegean Friends*, Red Hen Press, 2010), three other poetry anthologies besides *Rebel Angels*, and three books of essays (including *Voices, Places: Essays*, Paul Dry Books, 2018). He has also written libretti for the composers Lori Laitman and Tom Cipullo. His first poetry book, *The Buried Houses* (Story Line Press, 1991), won the Nicholas Roerich Prize. *The Sound: New and Selected Poems* (Red Hen Press) appeared in 2018. His most recent books are *Pacific Light: Poems* (Red Hen Press, 2023) and an essay collection, *Incarnation and Metamorphosis: Can Literature Change Us?* (Paul Dry Books), also from that year. Between 2010 and 2014, Mason was Colorado's poet laureate. A frequent contributor to the *Hudson Review*, he has taught at Minnesota State University Moorhead and Colorado College and currently lives in Tasmania.

G U S E V

from the story by Anton Chekhov

The wind has broken free of its chain.
The sea has neither sense nor pity,
and what befalls us falls like rain.
The water's hot as new-made jelly.

The sea has neither sense nor pity.
One dies while playing a game of cards.
The water's hot as new-made jelly.
Above it there are curious clouds.

One dies while playing a game of cards.
Pavel insists he is getting well.
Above the ship are curious clouds
like lions leaping over the swell.

Pavel insists he is getting well
and dies despising the peasant class.
Lions leaping over the swell
turn to scissors as they pass.

He dies despising the peasant class
while Gusev lies in a fevered state.
Clouds turn to scissors as they pass
and dead men find it hard to hate.

Gusev lies in a fevered state,
wishing he didn't have to die,
and though he finds it hard to hate
he's saddened when he sees the sky.

Wishing he didn't have to die,
he goes below to suffocate,
saddened now he's seen the sky.
He thinks of snow, the village gate,

and goes below to suffocate,
his dreams increasingly absurd.
He sleighs through snow, the village gate,
sleeps two days, dies on the third.

His dreams increasingly absurd,
he tosses the fever from his bed,
sleeps two days, dies on the third.
They sew the sail cloth over his head.

He tosses the fever from his bed.
The fever smiles and crawls back in.
They sew the sail cloth over his head.
Below deck someone's dying again.

The fever smiles and crawls back in.
The wind has broken free of its chain.
Below deck someone's dying again,
and what befalls us falls like rain.

SPOONING

After my grandfather died I went back home
to help my mother sell his furniture:
the old chair he did his sitting on,
the kitchen things. Going through his boxes
I found letters, cancelled checks, the usual
old photographs of relatives I hardly knew
and Grandmother, clutching an apron in both hands.

And *her*. There was an old publicity still
taken when she wore her hair like a helmet,
polished black. Posed before a cardboard shell
and painted waves, she seemed unattainable,
as she was meant to.

                                        For years we thought he lied
about his knowing her when he was young,
but Grandfather was a man who hated liars,
a man who worshipped all the tarnished virtues,
went daily to his shop at eight, until
the first of three strokes forced him to retire.

He liked talking. Somebody had to listen,
so I was the listener for hours after school
until my parents called me home to supper.
We'd sit on his glassed-in porch where he kept a box
of apples wrapped in newsprint.
He told me about the time he lost a job
at the mill. Nooksack seemed to kill its young
with boredom even then, but he owned a car,
a '24 Ford. He drove it east to see
America, got as far as Spokane's desert,
sold the car and worked back on the railroad.

Sometimes he asked me what I liked to do.
I told him about the drive-in movies where
my brother, Billy, took me if I paid.
In small towns movies are the only place to go.
Not Grandfather. He said they made them better when
nobody talked, and faces told it all.
"I knew Lydia Truman Gates," he said,
"back when she was plain old Lydia Carter
down on Water Street. One time her old man
caught us spooning out to the railroad tracks.
Nearly tanned my hide. He was a fisherman—
that is, till she moved her folks to Hollywood."

I don't know why, but I simply couldn't ask
what spooning was. He seemed to talk then
more to his chair's abrasions on the floor,
more to the pale alders outside his window.
The way he said her name I couldn't ask
who was Lydia Truman Gates.

"Nonsense,"
was all my mother said at dinner. "His mind
went haywire in the hospital. He's old.
He makes things up and can't tell the difference."
I think my father's smile embarrassed her
when he said, "The poor guy's disappointed.
Nothing ever went right for him, so he daydreams."

"Nonsense," my mother said. "And anyway
no Lydia Truman Gates ever came
from a town like this."

"It's not so bad a place.
I make a pretty decent living here."

My mother huffed. While I stared past my plate
Billy asked, "Who is Lydia Truman Gates?"

It wasn't long before we all found out.
The paper ran a story on her. How
she was famous in the twenties for a while,
married the oil billionaire, Gates, and retired.
She was coming back home to Nooksack. The mayor
would give a big award and ask her help
to renovate our landmark theater.

We had better things, our mother said, to spend
our money on than some old movie house,
though she remembered how it used to look.
She said that people living in the past
wouldn't amount to much.

We didn't tell our parents where we went
that night, riding our bikes in a warm wind
past the fish houses on the Puget Sound
and up Grace Street to the Hiawatha.
Inside, Billy held my hand, and showed me
faded paintings of Indians on the walls
and dark forest patterns in the worn carpet.
The place smelled stale like old decaying clothes
shut up in a trunk for twenty years,
but Nooksack's best were there, some in tuxes,
and women stuffed into their evening gowns.
We sat on the balcony looking down

on bald heads, high hairdos and jewels.
Near the stage they had a twenty-piece band—
I still remember when the lights went out
the violins rose like a flock of birds
all at once. The drums sounded a shudder.

We saw *Morocco Gold, The Outlaw, Colonel Clay*
and the comic short, *A Bird in the Hand*,
flickering down to the screen
where Lydia Truman Gates arose in veils,
in something gossamer
astonishing even in 1965.
Lydia Truman Gates was like a dream
of lithe attention, her dark eyes laughing
at death, at poverty or a satin bed.
And when they brought her on the stage, applause
rising and falling like a tidal wave,
I had to stand up on my seat to see
a frail old woman, assisted by two men,
tiny on that distant stage.

My brother
yanked me past what seemed like a hundred pairs
of knees for all the times I said "Excuse us."
We ran out where the chauffeur
waited by her limousine, his face painted
green by the light from Heilman's Piano Store,
breathing smoke. "You guys keep your distance."

"Is she coming out?"

He crushed his cigarette:
"No, she's gonna die in there. What do you think?"

More people joined us, pacing in the alley,
watching the chauffeur smoke by the door propped
open with a cinderblock.
And then the door half-opened, sighed back,
opened at last on the forearm of a man.

Behind him, Lydia Truman Gates stepped out
with her cane—hardly the woman I had seen
enduring all the problems of the world
with such aplomb. She stared down at the pavement,
saying, "Thank you, I can see it clearly now."

"Mrs. Gates," Billy stuttered. "Mrs. Gates."

The chauffeur tried to block us, but she said,
"That's all right, Andrew. They're just kids. I'm safe."

"Our grandpa says hello," I blurted out.

She paused for half a beat, glanced at Billy,
then peered at me as if to study terror,
smiling, "Well I'll be damned. And who's he?"

"Don't listen to him," Billy said. "He's nuts."

"George McCracken," I said, "the one you spooned with
down to the railroad tracks."

"George McCracken."
She straightened, looked up at the strip of sky.
"Spooned. Well, that's one way to talk about it."
She laughed from deep down in her husky lungs.
"Old Georgie McCracken. Is he still alive?
Too scared to come downtown and say hello?"

She reached out from her furs and touched my hair.
"Thanks for the message, little man. I knew him.
I knew he'd never get out of this town.
You tell your Grandpa Hi from Liddy Carter."

The man at her elbow said they had to leave.
She nodded, handing her award and purse
to the fat chauffeur.

                                        Then flashbulbs started popping.
I saw her face lit up, then pale and caving
back into the darkness. "Christ," she whispered,
"get me out of here."

                                        I stumbled, or was pushed.
My eyes kept seeing her exploding at me,
a woman made entirely of light
beside the smaller figure who was real.
Two men tipped her into the limousine
and it slid off like a shark, parting the crowd.

A picture ran in the next day's *Herald*—
the great actress touches a local boy.
For two weeks everybody talked about me,
but I kept thinking, *Is he still alive?*
Too scared to come downtown and say hello?

I thought of her decaying on a screen,
her ribs folding like a silk umbrella's rods,
while all the men who gathered around her
clutched at the remnants of her empty dress.

THE COLLECTOR'S TALE

When it was over I sat down last night,
shaken, and quite afraid I'd lost my mind.
The objects I have loved surrounded me
like friends in such composed society
they almost rid the atmosphere of fright.
I collected them, perhaps, as one inclined
to suffer other people stoically.

That's why, when I found Foley at my door—
not my shop, but here at my private home,
the smell of bourbon for his calling card—
I sighed and let him in without a word.
I'd only met the man two months before
and found his taste as tacky as they come,
his Indian ethic perfectly absurd.

The auction house in St. Paul where we met
was full that day of cherry furniture.
I still can't tell you why he'd chosen me
to lecture all about his Cherokee
obsessions, but I listened—that I regret.
My patience with a stranger's geniture
compelled him to describe his family tree.

He told me of his youth in Oklahoma,
his white father who steered clear of the Rez,
a grandma native healer who knew herbs
for every illness. Nothing like the 'burbs,
I guess. He learned to tell a real toma-
hawk from a handsaw, or lift his half-mad gaze
and "entertain" you with some acid barbs.

So he collected Indian artifacts,
the sort that sell for thousands in New York.
Beadwork, war shirts, arrowheads, shards of clay
beloved by dealers down in Santa Fe.
He lived to corner strangers, read them tracts
of his invention on the careful work
he would preserve and pridefully display.

Foley roamed the Great Plains in his van,
his thin hair tied back in a ponytail,
and people learned that he was smart enough
to deal. He made a living off this stuff,
became a more authenticated man.
But when he drank he would begin to rail
against the white world's trivializing fluff.

Last night when he came in, reeking of smoke
and liquor, gesticulating madly
as if we'd both returned from the same bar,
I heard him out a while, the drunken bore,
endured his leaning up against my oak
credenza there, until at last I gladly
offered him a drink and a kitchen chair.

I still see him, round as a medicine ball
with a three-day beard, wearing his ripped jeans
and ratty, unlaced Nikes without socks.
I see him searching through two empty packs
and casting them aside despite my scowl,
opening a third, lighting up—he careens
into my kitchen, leaving boozy tracks.

I offered brandy. He didn't mind the brand
or that I served it in a water glass.
He drank with simple greed, making no show
of thanks, and I could see he wouldn't go.
He told me nothing had happened as he planned,
how he left Rasher's tiny shop a mess.
I killed him, Foley said. *You've got to know.*

You know the place. Grand Avenue. The Great
White Way they built over my people's bones
after the western forts made stealing safe.
Safe for that fucking moneyed generation
F. Scott Fitzgerald used to write about—
and here was Rasher, selling off such crap
no self-respecting dealer'd waste his time.

I heard he had good beadwork, Chippewa,
but when I sent in all I saw was junk.
I'm thinking, Christ, the neighbors here must love him,
the one dusty-shuttered place on the block
and inside, counters filled with silver plate
so tarnished nobody would touch it, irons
with fraying cords and heaps of magazines.

He had the jawbone of a buffalo
from South Dakota, an old Enfield rifle,
a barn chair (or a cut-rate replica),
German bible, a blue-eyed Jesus framed
in bottle caps—I mean he had everything
but paint-by-number sunsets, so much junk
I bet he hadn't made a sale in years.

You got to know this guy—skinny bald head
and both his hands twisted from arthritis.
I wouldn't give his place a second look
except I heard so much about this beadwork.
He leads me to a case in the back room.
I take a look. The stuff is fucking new,
pure Disneyland, not even off the Rez.

Foley's glass was empty: I poured him more
to buy time while I thought of some excuse
to get him out of here. If homicide
indeed were his odd tale's conclusion, I'd
rather let him pass out on my floor,
then dash upstairs and telephone the police.
I wouldn't mind if "fucking" Foley fried.

It's crap, he said. *I tell this slimy coot*
he doesn't know an Indian from a dog.
I can't believe I drove five hundred miles
to handle sentimental tourist crap.
He rolled himself upright in my kitchen chair
and looked at me with such complete disdain
that I imagined Mr. Rasher's stare.

I knew the man. We dealers somehow sense
who we trust and who the characters are.
I looked at my inebriated guest
and saw the fool-as-warrior on a quest
for the authentic, final recompense
that would rub out, in endless, private war,
all but his own image of the best.

Pretty quick I see I hurt his feelings.
He gets all proud on me and walks around
pointing at this and that,
a World's Fair pin, a Maris autograph,
and then he takes me to a dark wood cupboard
and spins the combination on the lock
and shows me what's inside. The old man

shows me his motherfucking pride and joy.
I look inside his cupboard and it's there
all right—a black man's head with eyes sewn shut—
I mean this fucker's real, all dried and stuffed,
a metal ashtray planted in the skull.
I look and it's like the old man's nodding,
Yeah, yeah, you prick, now tell me this is nothing.

He's looking at me looking at this head,
telling me he found it in a house
just up the street. Some dead white guy's estate
here in the liberal north allowed this coot
whatever his twisted little hands could take,
and then he hoards it away for special guests.
I didn't say a thing. I just walked out.

Now Foley filled his glass, drinking it down.
His irises caught fire as he lit up.
I sat across from him and wiped my palms
but inside I was setting off alarms
as if I should alert this sleeping town
that murder lived inside it. I could stop
the story now, I thought, but nothing calms

a killer when he knows he must confess,
and Foley'd chosen me to hear the worst.
Weird, he said, looking straight at me beyond
his burning cigarette. *I got so mad.*
Like all I thought of was a hundred shelves
collecting dust in Rasher's shop, and how
a dead man's head lay at the center of it.

I had to get a drink. Some yuppie bar
that charged a fortune for its cheapest bourbon.
I'm in there while the sun sets on the street
and people drop in after leaving work.
I look at all these happy people there—
laughing, anyway; maybe they aren't happy—
the well-dressed women tossing back their hair,

the men who loosen their designer ties
and sip their single malts—living on bones
of other people, right?
And two blocks down the street, in Rasher's shop,
a head where someone flicked his ashes once,
because of course a darky can't be human,
and someone's family kept that darky's head.

These genteel people with their decent souls
must have been embarrassed finding it,
and Rasher got it for a fucking song
and even he could never sell the thing.
No, he showed it to me just to get me,
just to prove I hadn't seen it all.
Well, he was right, I hadn't seen it all.

I didn't know the worst that people do
could be collected like a beaded bag,
bad medicine or good, we keep the stuff
and let it molder in our precious cases.
Some fucker cared just how he dried that head
and stitched the skin and cut the hole in the top—
big medicine for a man who liked cigars.

It's just another piece of history,
human, like a slave yoke or a scalping knife,
and maybe I was drunk on yuppie booze,
but I knew some things had to be destroyed.
Hell, I could hardly walk, but I walked back,
knocked on Rasher's door until he opened,
pushed him aside like a bag of raked-up leaves.

Maybe I was shouting, I don't know.
I heard him shouting at my back, and then
he came around between me and the case,
a little twisted guy with yellow teeth
telling me he'd call the fucking cops.
I found the jawbone of that buffalo.
I mean I must have picked it up somewhere,

maybe to break the lock, but I swung hard
and hit that old fucker upside the head
and he went down so easy I was shocked.
He lay there moaning in a spreading pool
I stepped around. I broke that old jawbone
prizing the lock, but it snapped free, and I
snatched out the gruesome head.

I got it to my van all right, and then
went back to check on Rasher. He was dead.
For a while I tried to set his shop on fire
to see the heaps of garbage in it burn,
but you'd need gasoline to get it going
and besides, I couldn't burn away the thought
of that weird thing I took from there tonight.

It's out there, Foley said. *I'm parked outside*
a few blocks down—I couldn't find your house.
I knew you'd listen to me if I came.
I knew you'd never try to turn me in.
You want to see it? No? I didn't either,
and now I'll never lose that goddamned head,
even if I bury it and drive away.

By now the bluster'd left his shrinking frame
and I thought he would vomit in my glass,
but Foley had saved strength enough to stand,
while I let go of everything I'd planned—
the telephone, police, and bitter fame
that might wash over my quiet life and pass
away at some inaudible command.

I thought of all the dead things in my shop.
No object I put up was poorly made.
Nothing of mine was inhumane, although
I felt death in a kind of undertow
pulling my life away. *Make it stop,*
I thought, as if poor Foley had betrayed
our best ideals. Of course I let him go.

The truth is, now he's left I feel relieved.
I locked the door behind him, but his smell
has lingered in my hallway all these hours.
I've mopped the floor, washed up, moved pots of flowers
to places that he touched. If I believed,
I would say Foley had emerged from hell.
I ask for help, but the silent house demurs.

Patricia Smith (b. 1955)

Drawing from her personal archive of daguerreotypes, tintypes, and vintage photos, Patricia Smith's most recent book, *Unshuttered* (TriQuarterly Books/Northwestern University Press, 2023), uses lyric poetry and dramatic monologues to animate the anonymous Black men, women, and children whose images she has collected. "Edith's Sestina" and "Siblings," the two poems below, both appear in Smith's 2008 collection, *Blood Dazzler* (Coffee House Press), a National Book Award finalist that tracks the evolution of Hurricane Katrina, which ravaged New Orleans in August of 2005. Although the first poem is a dramatic monologue, it doubles as narrative because of the framing device of Smith's prefatory note, and because of the cataclysmic event that befalls the speaker, attenuating her cry for help.

Born in Chicago, Smith received the Ruth Lilly Poetry Prize for Lifetime Achievement in 2021. Her 2017 collection, *Incendiary Art* (TriQuarterly Books/Northwestern University Press), won the Kingsley Tufts Poetry Award, a *Los Angeles Times* Book Prize, and a NAACP Image Award. It was also a finalist for the Pulitzer Prize. *Shoulda Been Jimi Savannah* (Coffee House Press, 2012) earned the Lenore Marshall Poetry Prize from the Academy of American Poets, while an earlier book, *Teahouse of the Almighty* (Coffee House Press, 2006), was a National Poetry Series selection. She is a four-time champion of the National Poetry Slam. Her other laurels include the Rebekah Johnson Bobbitt National Prize for Poetry from the Library of Congress and fellowships from the Guggenheim Foundation and the National Endowment for the Arts.

With the scholar and novelist Charles Johnson, Smith coauthored *Africans in America: America's Journey through Slavery* (Houghton Mifflin Harcourt) in 1998, the year of her controversial departure from journalism. More recently, she edited the crime fiction anthology *Staten Island Noir* (Akashic Books, 2021). Her own contribution to that volume had been chosen in 2013 for the *Best American Mystery Stories* anthology. Today she is a distinguished professor at City University of New York (College of Staten Island), a visiting professor of creative writing at Princeton University, and a faculty member of the Vermont College of Fine Arts' Postgraduate Writers' Conference.

ETHEL'S SESTINA

Ethel Freeman's body sat for days in her wheelchair outside the New Orleans Convention Center. Her son Herbert, who had assured his mother that help was on the way, was forced to leave her there once she died.

Gon' be obedient in this here chair,
gon' bide my time, fanning against this sun.
I ask my boy, and all he says is *Wait*.
He wipes my brow with steam, says I should sleep.
I trust his every word. Herbert my son.
I believe him when he says help gon' come.

Been so long since all these suffrin' folks come
to this place. Now on the ground 'round my chair,
they sweat in my shade, keep asking my son
could that be a bus they see. It's the sun
foolin' them, shining much too loud for sleep,
making us hear engines, wheels. Not yet. Wait.

Lawd, some folks prayin' for rain while they wait,
forgetting what rain can do. When it come,
it smashes living flat, wakes you from sleep,
eats streets, washes you clean out of the chair
you be sittin' in. Best to praise this sun,
shinin' its dry shine. *Lawd have mercy, son,*

is it coming? Such a strong man, my son.
Can't help but believe when he tells us, *Wait.*
Wait some more. Wish some trees would block this sun.
We wait. Ain't no white men or buses come,
but look—see that there? Get me out this chair,
help me stand on up. No time for sleepin',

cause look what's rumbling this way. If you sleep
you gon' miss it. *Look there*, I tell my son.
He don't hear. I'm 'bout to get out this chair,
but the ghost in my legs tells me to wait,
wait for the salvation that's sho to come.
I see my savior's face 'longside that sun.

Nobody sees me running toward the sun.
Lawd, they think I done gone and fell asleep.
They don't hear *Come.*

Come.
Come.
Come.
Come.
Come.
Come.
Ain't but one power make me leave my son.
I can't wait, Herbert. Lawd knows I can't wait.
Don't cry, boy, I ain't in that chair no more.

Wish you coulda come on this journey, son,
seen that ol' sweet sun lift me out of sleep.
Didn't have to wait. And see my golden chair?

SIBLINGS

Hurricanes, 2005

Arlene learned to dance backwards in heels that were too high.
Bret prayed for a shaggy mustache made of mud and hair.
Cindy just couldn't keep her windy legs together.
Dennis never learned to swim.
Emily whispered her gusts into a thousand skins.
Franklin, farsighted and anxious, bumbled villages.
Gert spat her matronly name against a city's flat face.
Harvey hurled a wailing child high.
Irene, the baby girl, threw pounding tantrums.
José liked the whip sound of slapping.
Lee just craved the whip.
Maria's thunder skirts flew high when she danced.
Nate was mannered and practical. He stormed precisely.
Ophelia nibbled weirdly on the tips of depressions.
Philippe slept too late, flailing on a wronged ocean.
Rita was a vicious flirt. She woke Philippe with rumors.
Stan was born business, a gobbler of steel.
Tammy crooned country, getting the words all wrong.
Vince died before anyone could remember his name.
Wilma opened her maw wide, flashing rot.

None of them talked about Katrina.
She was their odd sister,
the blood dazzler.

Joseph Harrison (1957–2024)

The following poem is taken from Joseph Harrison's final single volume, *Sometimes I Dream I Am Walt Whitman* (2020), published by Waywiser Press, for which he served as North American editor. Waywiser has brought out most of Harrison's oeuvre, including *Shakespeare's Horse* (2015), *Someone Else's Name* (2003)—both finalists for the Poets' Prize—*Identity Theft* (2008), and *Collected Poems* in 2024. With Damiano Abeni, he edited poems by John Ashbery (1927–2017) for an Italian edition: *Un mondo che non può essere migliore* (Luca Sossella Editore, 2008). The book received the Special Prize from the Premio Napoli. Harrison, who administered Waywiser's Anthony Hecht Poetry Prize, was also editor of *The Hecht Prize Anthology* (Waywiser Press, 2010). He was honored with a Guggenheim fellowship and an Academy Award in Literature from the American Academy of Arts and Letters.

In a tribute to the literary critic Harold Bloom (1930–2019), Harrison wrote of his own aesthetic: "my whole sense of intertextuality, an important component of what I do, is influenced by his analysis of the hidden dynamics between poems" ("Remembering Harold Bloom," *Literary Matters*, Winter 2020). "If one is condemned to be a ventriloquist," he adds, "one might as well embrace it." While an undergraduate at Yale University, he had taken a course with Bloom on contemporary American poetry. Harrison went on to earn a master of arts degree from Johns Hopkins University, and he settled in Baltimore, Maryland, teaching, editing, and writing. He was born in Richmond, Virginia.

DICKENS ON FIRE

Precipitate, determined, absolute
In bending all around him to his will,
    Inflammable and volatile
        And furiously driven,
    Prone to pity and self-pity,
        Oblivious yet acute,
Cruel to his wife, kind to the destitute,
            A man of style
                And skill
        And fueled propensity
    To slog on mile by soggy mile
    Crackling with charged intensity,
            And all the while
Keen eyes fixed on the goals toward which he'd striven,
Fame and its fortunes, charity, Gad's Hill,

Dickens was steadied, somewhat, by routine
Keeping his reckless energy on track,
    A morning shower, quick, ice-cold,
        Then breakfast, then ascending
    To wrestle at his writing desk
        With how to set the scene
For tension, sentiment, an unforeseen
            And manifold
                Attack
        Of twists and turns, grotesque
    Incinerations, crimes of old,
    Kind quirks that verge on the burlesque
            Just as they're told
To move the heart, and move it toward an ending,
To keep the pages turning to the back,

(Not to imply his urgent fluency
Spared him the chosen trials of the trade,

The fundamental restlessness,
Dead hours, dead days, dead weeks,
The sharp downspirals of depression
And pained uncertainty,
The getting up then coming back to see
What little mess
We've made
Or haven't, the obsession
Guttering till our dark distress
Snuffs out another hapless session
Where more is less,
When skies clear, from the valleys rise the peaks,
The dam breaks and the images cascade),

Then stop for lunch, done writing for the day
At two or three, and after a hearty feed
Launch vigorous activity,
A long and fast-paced walk
Through fields and lanes, or streets and parks,
Then home to, fiercely, play
At cricket, pocket billiards, or croquet,
And after tea
Proceed
With more communal larks,
As brisk conviviality
Strikes brilliant conversational sparks,
Civility
Brings drink and food and funny games and talk
All wreathed in smoke, according to his need,

Or, if he had the numbers, organize
His family and friends into a troupe
To take a part and break a leg
For dramaturgic purpose,

Staging whatever he'd select
While he would scrutinize
And drill the children, prompt and tyrannize
(But never beg)
The group
To quickening effect,
As he, both fuse and powder keg,
Would blaze away, and thus infect
Augustus Egg
And Forster and Frank Stone and Uncle Porpoise
Till they would conquer, since they must not stoop,

Or drop by places where he'd find his friends,
The Athenaeum, or the Parthenon,
The Garrick, where the smoke was thick
And he could have his say
Among the clubby tight connections
Frank *bonhomie* extends,
Denounce what someone mindlessly defends
Or parry *Sic*
Et Non,
Discuss the next elections,
The latest play, the lunatic
Love-muddled slapstick indirections
Of some sidekick
As, effervescent, wired, on high display,
The Sparkler sparkled evenings, on and on,

Or supervise a testimonial
Dinner to benefit some heartfelt cause,
Old actors or the Ragged Schools,
Reforming prostitutes,
Clean water and less filthy air
(His ceremonial

Issues were native, not colonial),
            To torch the fools'
                Dumb laws
        (Sunday restrictions) where
    Flammable, drain the worst cesspools,
    Build decent housing (Columbia Square),
            Rhetorical tools
Full bore, "Thanks to you all, thanks to Miss Coutts,"
A last drumroll, the punchline, the applause,

Though for long stretches he would spend his days
On one consuming project (still in his prime,
    Or so he thought, strength could be found,
        Plus he had many bills),
    Like editing a magazine
        For fiction, reviews of plays,
Opinionated letters, brave essays
            To clear the ground,
                The grime,
        The soot, to fix the scene,
    So *Household Words*, then *All the Year Round*
    Would flash together, burnished clean
            And market-bound,
With help from his assistant, W. H. Wills,
Another number, ship-shape, out on time,

Or dragging his Dramatic Company
On tour again (no other thrill would suffice—
    He missed the stage lights, burned to go,
        And tickets always sold
    For amateur theatricals
        Where a happy few could see
A cast of odd, esteemed celebrity
            Braving the snow
                And ice

To not turn cannibals
Despite *The Frozen Deep*), just so
Feeling would fill the meeting halls
And only grow
To warm his Wardour, dying in the cold,
Rapt with the ardors of self-sacrifice,

And then there were the constant public readings
That drove and drained him through his latter years,
So lucrative, he would insist
He must go on despite
Exhaustion, bravely take the stage
For ritual proceedings
(Doctors objected, he ignored their pleadings,
Proudly dismissed
Their fears),
The great man of the age
A spectacle (as he'd persist
The characters leapt off the page)
Not to be missed,
The desk, the hat, the gloves, the even light,
The sure crescendo, the held breath, the cheers,

All so addictive, apple of every eye,
Charley was their darling, he was adored,
They found it riveting, sublime,
Loved the trial in *Pickwick*,
Loved to pity the little tykes
Like Copperfield, whose "I"
Was him, and Tiny Tim, "who did NOT die"
This Christmastime
(They roared),
Shuddered in fear when Sikes
Would finish Nancy one more time

(She pleads, he lifts the club, he strikes,
He flees the crime)
As, murderer and murdered, he felt sick,
His body suffered as their spirits soared,

Then, too, because of or despite it all,
The man was always moving, in nervous flight
From boredom or mortality,
To witness, sundry-wise,
The elemental earthly show,
Summoned by the call
Of roaring water to watch Niagara fall
All majesty
And might
Shimmer-spanned by rainbow
After rainbow, ceaselessly
Crashing a hundred feet below,
Where he could see
Tremendous ghosts of spray and mist arise,
Veils of the first things, darkness, depth, God, light,

Or drawn to clamber, one sharp winter night,
Accompanied by guides, his pregnant wife,
Georgina, "Pickle," a fat stranger,
Up Mount Vesuvius,
Intentionally starting late
To climb in fading light
(He timed it to the moonrise, it was tight)
Despite all danger
To life
And limb, as if dumb fate
Were some benevolent arranger,
Though told they really shouldn't wait
He wouldn't change or

Waver, pressed on ("Good Lord deliver us,"
The sherpas prayed) as wind cut like a knife,

The litters with the women in them veered,
The porters stumbled, cursing, shrieked advice,
   The fat man's litter wobbled, hovered,
      While, creeping, up they went
   (Descent posed the real risk of falling,
      When Pickle disappeared,
Slipping right down a slope that, as he feared,
         Was slickly covered
            In ice,
      Wildly cannonballing
   Out of sight, to be recovered),
   Up where a smoke-filled, sulfurous, appalling
         Plain discovered
Gigantic cinders, with flakes of fire, hell-sent,
Rained down to scorch an anti-paradise,

And where great sheets of flame streamed forth he must,
True to his own wild way, rashly ascend
   To see the molten crater churning,
      Must crawl right to the brim
   And, singeing, linger there (although
      He found having to trust
His weight to the thinness of the trembling crust
         A touch concerning),
            Suspend-
      ed, boiling gulf below,
   Then, giddy, roll back down, returning
   Blackened, smoking from head to toe,
         His clothes still burning,
But all in every moment, being him,
Dickens on fire, as always, right to the end.

Catherine Tufariello (b. 1963)

Born in Ithaca, New York, Catherine Tufariello earned a bachelor's degree from the State University of New York, Buffalo, where her father was a chemistry professor and dean. Following receipt of a PhD from Cornell University, she taught there and at College of Charleston, University of Miami, and, finally, Valparaiso University. She then exchanged an academic career for one of a community mental health provider. At present, she is a student counselor at the University of Oklahoma Health Sciences Center. Author of the chapbooks *Annunciations* (Oak Knoll Books, 2001) and *Free Time* (Robert L. Barth, 2011), Tufariello published a full-length collection, *Keeping My Name* (Texas Tech University) in 2004. The volume won several honors, including the Poets' Prize and a designation as a Booklist Editors' Choice and finalist for a *Los Angeles Times* Book Prize.

Her poem "February 18, 1943" commemorates the day that Hans Scholl (1918–43) and Sophie Scholl (1921–43), brother and sister, were arrested by the Gestapo for distributing anti-Nazi leaflets at the University of Munich, as part of the White Rose resistance movement. Four days later, they were executed by guillotine, along with Christoph Probst (1919–43).

FEBRUARY 18, 1943

In memory of Hans and Sophie Scholl,
leaders of the White Rose student resistance movement,
executed February 22, 1943.

I imagine how easily you could have gotten away,
Standing in the Ludwigstraße in the sun
That improbably springlike February day,
The not-quite empty suitcase slung
Between you—like two students on holiday,
Let out of class, on your way to catch a train.
Relieved and out of breath,
You stood for a moment blinking in the sun,
Tasting the early spring that caught all Munich unawares
After bleak weeks of cold.
How hopeful the light must have looked, how far from death.
Was it that you suddenly felt young?
—Another nose-thumbing at the omnipotent State!
Or was it the recklessness of the desperate?
Not furtively, but in the pale spun-gold
Of full daylight, like farmers casting grain,
You'd left your leaflets scattered on the floors
In the hallways, on the windowsills, at the doors
Of the lecture rooms, and, ignoring their stony stares,
In the marble laps of Ludwig and Leopold.
Was it the change in weather
That made your glances catch, a glance that said
Almost gaily, *Why waste any?* so that instead
Of slipping away as planned, you raced together
Back to the empty hall,
And up the stairs, to let the last ones fall?

I imagine, then, how you leaned from the great height
Of the gallery railing into a well of light;
How, giddy with boldness and vertigo,
You popped the latch, and—hurriedly this time—scooped
The leftover handfuls out.
For a few seconds, the pages must have swooped
Like wind-torn blossoms, sideways in the air,
Filling the gallery with a storm of white,
While under the skylight with its square of blue
Your arms were still flung wide;
And while, rounding a corner down below,
For just a moment, the porter, Jakob Schmid,
Must have stopped to stare,
Not indignant yet, but merely shocked,
Blinded for an instant by the glare,
Before he recovered himself and did
His job as he'd been taught;
Before milling students spilled into the hall
From morning lectures, but not quite fast enough;
Before Schmid gave a shout,
And surging forward in the tumult, caught
The dark-haired young man's shoulder in a rough
Policeman's grip that would not be shaken off,
Though he didn't try, and the girl stayed by his side;
Before, in a sudden hush, the crowd withdrew,
And the doors all locked.

David Yezzi (b. 1966)

David Yezzi's most recent book is *Late Romance: Anthony Hecht—A Poet's Life* (St. Martin's Press, 2023). In Yezzi's narrative and lyric poems, one often perceives the biographer's debt to his subject. Yezzi mines the same metrical resources, and the same veins of irony, as did Hecht (1923–2004), and not infrequently attains the other's visionary awe. Yezzi's verse collections include *More Things in Heaven: New and Selected Poems* (Measure Press, 2022), *Black Sea* (Carnegie Mellon University Press, 2018), and *Birds of the Air* (Carnegie Mellon University Press, 2013), a finalist for the Poets' Prize. An earlier volume, *Azores* (Swallow Press/Ohio University Press, 2008), was chosen by *Slate* as a "Best Book" of the year. His first full collection, *The Hidden Model* (TriQuarterly/Northwestern University Press), appeared in 2003.

Born in Albany, New York, Yezzi earned an undergraduate degree in theater from Carnegie Mellon University, and an MFA in creative writing from Columbia University. In 1998, he was a Wallace Stegner Fellow at Stanford University. Alongside his poetic development, Yezzi has cultivated careers in teaching and literary journalism, serving variously as director of the Unterberg Poetry Center of the 92nd Street Y in New York City, as executive editor and poetry editor of *The New Criterion*, and as editor of the *Hopkins Review*. He is a professor in the Writing Seminars at Johns Hopkins University and was named a Guggenheim fellow in 2025.

Apart from teaching and editing, and the writing of essays, reviews, libretti, and poetry, Yezzi is—as the second entry below demonstrates—entrenched in a life of theater. A cofounder of Thick Description, a theater company in San Francisco, he still acts: in 2021, he played the title role of King Lear for the Baltimore Shakespeare Factory. In 2022, he appeared as the Ghost and Player King in Chesapeake Shakespeare Company's production of *Hamlet*, and, the next year as Charles Dickens in the group's adaptation of *A Christmas Carol*. His one-act verse play *Schnauzer* (Exot Books, 2018) has been staged by the Baltimore Poets Theatre. "Dirty Dan," directly below, addresses fellow poet Tom Disch (1940–2008). Along with other of his verse monologues, the poem has been performed at the Bowery Poetry Club in New York City.

DIRTY DAN

for Tom Disch

I can't remember what the night was like.
It was *phssh*, twenty- . . . seven? years ago,
before I even knew you. I was home,
from college maybe, hanging out with friends?
Christmas break, it must have been. And cold.
Too bad you never saw him. Too late now,
not just because there's no way Dirty Dan
is still alive (he was ancient, even then),
but more because you are not, so prematurely . . .

So: Dan. I only saw him once. Just once,
I guess that's part of it. It snowed that night.
(Let's pretend that we're both sitting around
in your living room, just telling stories.)
Now, it's my turn, right? So — Dirty Dan.
I swear to god this guy was unbelievable:
this wiry geezer, bug eyed, in a toque,
white short-sleeve chef shirt and a stubble beard.
But wait, hold on, back up. So, this is Dan:
a short-order cook with ice blue, staring eyes . . .
I need to tell you a bit about before.
At any rate, it's late one night, and I'm
home from school on break. I'm seeing friends
and drunk and underage and talking "art"
with Julie and her boyfriend Mitch, who's just
like a miniature professor with bad skin.
He's smart and tweedy and totally insane,
and also so completely full of shit,
which I like. And mostly he likes books,

and getting stoned and talking late. Talk, talk.
And then, long-suffering Julie, small and preppy,
and really very cute, I think sometimes.

One minute, Mitch is spouting Joyce — about
how all he actually wanted was to write
a really good read crammed with lots of jokes
for all his friends to savor, to make them laugh.
Next: the neon blur and flat pink light
of a diner by the park.
                                            I remember this:
the snow and cold and Mitch rubbing his hands
together, as he says, "Let's go see Dan,"
then we're in a booth.
                                            The place is packed.
It's 3 a.m., and there must be a dozen
booths like ours. The counter's jammed with kids
who've come from Luna, dancing, high and freeze-framed
in strobe flashes and ethereal black light.
And now they're beat and hungry, after-hours,
giving up their orders to these guys,
also kids, who write down all the coffee
and toast and juice and ham and bacon sides,
the eggs — fried, scrambled, over easy, up —
and call then out across the room to Dan.
Our voices mingle in the greasy air,
talking bullshit, screaming with delight,
goofing, over which the waiters' voices
fly like homing birds,
                                            while, at the grill,
Dan shuttles like a Chinese acrobat,
balancing every order in his mind
like so many plates spun on wooden dowels,
never dropping one, and grunting out

he'd got the order, pick up twenty-one.
And we were there to watch. And snarl-haired Mitch,
who, I just remembered, lost a tooth,
or, no, he had a denture he'd remove
that left this gaping hole each time he'd laugh.
We laughed all night that night.
                                        That's why we got
together in the first place, why we drank
and smoked and talked of books. That's why we went
to see Dan in his kitchen, to be amazed,
the way that the whole diner was amazed,
the way the kids who took the orders were amazed.
Dirty Dan was this incredible
freaking genius. Brilliant. You think it's easy?
Try it. What he did was just not something
anyone can do: he knew it, too.
You could tell. How he could yell in a rage
When two of the kid waiters talked at once,
screwing up his groove — and they'd apologize,
since the last thing they wanted to do was break
his perfect streak that ran till 5 a.m.
It was like riding down the trough of a wave
that started somewhere out in the Pacific.
God, how we roared. That's all we really wanted
was to laugh.
                        And you were like that, too, I guess.
That's the way it always went, wasn't it?
Open the wine, talk books, and reel off new jokes
that always had some place inside the flow
of a larger conversation for the night,
and a place, too, in breaking the tick, tick
of dingy sink, cold coffee, quiet phone,
afternoon nap, and too much television,

which haunted you in daylight till the night
came back and, ranting, after-hours, we'd people
the vastness with our stories and we'd laugh.

Now you're dead, I wonder more and more
whom I should tell them to, stories like this,
running through them in my head mostly.
Julie and Mitch? *Pfft*. I can't really say
what happened to them. Did they ever marry?
I doubt it.
Julie must have had more sense than that.
Don't get me wrong; Mitch was my friend, too.
(He was the one who called him Dirty Dan,
cackling and growling with his gap-tooth grin.)
We were a lot alike.
Now I don't know where they are. Alive?
Somewhere? Nowhere?
                                        Too long ago to know. I laugh
a lot less with them gone. Does that surprise you?

TOMORROW & TOMORROW

A travesty

I.
"What's done cannot be undone."

Am I right?
So . . . obvious. So irrefutable.
Of course, if it is done it can't be undone.
Any idiot knows that. Or else:
"If it were done, when 'tis done, then 'twere well
it were done quickly."
"When the hurly-burly's done."
"Is execution done in Cawdor?"
"Yet let that be
Which the eye fears, when it is done, to see."
You see? Stuff happens, you can't take it back.
Just one of those things you don't have to say,
but sometimes we still need reminding of:
"What's done is done." So good, it's like a spell,
a charm, a bell: *done, done*. But Lady Macbeth?
She wasn't the only one who said it; no,
others said it. Sophocles, for instance,
he said it, something like it; said it long
before her, if you want to know the truth.
Lots of people said it, and it's true.

I did that play, a million years ago.
And every night I'd listen from the wings
and hear those lines.
I was an actor. Sort of.
Or, technically, more like a waiter. So,

I'd pick up part-time shifts behind the bar,
serving Mai Tais underneath the whale
at the American Museum of Natural History —
revolving-door jobs in the service industry
broken up by brief forays on stage.
Here's a couple more, in case you missed it:
"In every point twice done and then done double."
"I have done no harm."
                                        (That's what they always say.)

The show was a disaster. Every night,
we died a dozen deaths on different stages.
Macbeth and Lady, they were really married,
married in real life, and they produced it.
In Germany — in English but in Germany.
In western Germany before the wall
came down.
                        The other waiters were so excited
when they heard I got a job, that I was Malcolm,
they bought me drinks and gave me this old book:
a beat-up phrase book unearthed at the Strand,
Berlitz or something, and completely worthless.
It must have been from fifty years ago.
Oh, and it had lots of useful stuff,
like "Es tut mir leid, ich brach meine Platte,"
which means, I think, "I'm sorry, I broke my plate,"
or other things I probably would need
like "Ist es Zeit für meine Spritze?":
"Is it time for my injection?"
I remember looking over at my girlfriend
just then — Sasha, a dancer. That made her laugh.
Her teeth were too big and a bit off-center
in a way that made me always want to kiss her.
                                        "I go, and it is done;
the bell invites me."

Before we left, we froze our asses off:
rehearsing in some empty public school
on 6th and B — no heat and no hot water,
when people slept in tents in Tompkins Square.
Kids would throw M-80s off the roofs —
these huge explosions — and we'd have to run for it.
We'd step outside to smoke a cigarette,
and they'd come streaming down like, *holy shit!*
By dark, the place cleared out:
syringes in the walkups, random gun-pops,
vials strewn in doorways like bright glass
from a car wreck.
So, I told my waiting job
so long and stuffed a backpack full of clothes.
I can't remember what we said that morning,
Sasha and I. There's lots I don't remember.
Though some of it's still there, a skin, invisible.
Some things you never quite recover from.
I left. So what was I supposed to do?

You know the curse?
You're not supposed to say the word *Macbeth*;
instead you say the "Scottish Tragedy,"
which sounds ridiculous, but there you have it.
Let's say we're talking in the dressing room,
and I say the name Macbeth, you know, accidentally.
Actors have this thing, they have this code
(or not a code; it's more of a behavior):
I'm supposed to go outside and close the door.
I turn around three times, say *shit* or *fuck!*
and then I knock and ask to come back in.
It's kind of cool, 'cause then it's like a safety,
like canceling something bad: you take it back.
But cursed? Do people ever think they are?

Who thinks they're cursed? You think, well that's not good,
or that's a string of bad luck, a bad year,
but no one thinks they're cursed. Not at the time.

The play was bad, no doubt.
                                        It wasn't that.
Some things just sort of happened. Little things
at first, annoying stuff, like props gone missing.
But then we crashed the van: Lady Macbeth
was driving. She spun out on the Autobahn
and had to do the tour in a cast —
"Out damned spot . . ." She'd start rubbing the plaster,
night after night, sleepwalking, in a trance.
And after that I did begin to think
that maybe we were cursed. It felt like that,
like we'd done something wrong.
                                        It tells you things
that you don't want to know — about yourself,
about how you think that everything is fine,
then one cold morning with the snow outside
you wake up sweating from an awful dream,
convinced that you have done things so unspeakable . . .
What if you did, only you didn't know it?
Or, more likely, knew it, and forgot.
Something you'd never believe in a thousand years:
murder your father, sleep with your own mother,
those kind of things.
But that's a different play.

II.

This is the way the line's supposed to go.
The battle's over, right? We won: our side.
And Banquo spends the night in Macbeth's castle.

He gets there and looks up and sees this swift
nesting among the rafters there. This scarred
old warrior, this patriarch of kings
is so moved by the sight of this, he makes
a joke about the song birds having sex.
He sniffs the air and says:
                                        This guest of summer,
The temple-haunting martlet, does approve,
By the loved mansionry, that the heaven's breath
Smells wooingly here; no jutty, frieze,
Buttress, nor coign of vantage, but this bird
Hath made his pendent bed and procreant cradle.
Where they must breed and haunt, I have observ'd
The air is delicate.
                              Something like that.
So, our guy comes.
                                        Our Banquo's name is Bill,
and Bill's this graying hippy from the Village,
who pays a dollar-fifty rent, he says,
which frees him up to do a bit of acting.
So, Bill comes out; he looks up in the grid,
with three or four of us just standing there,
and Duncan, who's the king, so hugely fat
he's like a minivan. So, Bill looks up.
(He's downstage.) He looks down. He looks at us:
"This . . . bird," he says.
                                        And he's completely up:
that's when you're off the script, you're up, you're *up*.
You've no idea who you are or what
you're doing.
                    It's, I guess, a bit like drowning,
like being under water, but too deep.
You go into a kind of panic mode —
the world slows down and hangs there at a distance.

From the cold murky bottom you look up
and see the small disk of the sun receding,
and you realize you haven't got the air
to get back up. So you begin to swim,
then lose your bearings in a cloud of bubbles.
King Duncan sees this — Duncan's name is Neil —
Duncan sees that Bill's completely jammed,
so what he does is . . . throw the guy a bone?
Skip ahead and pick up later on?
No, no. He stands there, doesn't say a word,
steps forward even, sort of cranes his neck,
as if to say, "Uh-huh? We're list-en-ing."
I tell you, actors — they're a pack of dogs,
completely warped.
                                        Still, it was all good fun.
Lady's in a cast, the show's a bomb.
Not even knowing German, we could tell
the papers thought we were a total joke.
But we were getting paid and seeing sights
and drinking beer. A lot.

I can't forget that show, and not because
I was the freest then or wildest or whatever;
just, parts of it keep coming back that way.
Or, earlier:
                              It's snowing. We're on Jane Street,
with wood smoke rising from the townhouses.
Sasha's in lace-up boots and woolen tights,
short skirt from which her dancer's legs
are shooshing in the cold.
She's pouting over something, and I'm hanging
on every word and sigh, on every turn
of her moods, and there are many, same as me.

Across the avenue, up sagging steps
to a tiny place she shared with another girl.
The roommate hated me, 'cause every night
we'd show up late then quickly disappear
into the bedroom — closet, crawl space, lair,
barely enough to squeeze a mattress in —
and close the door and make love with the lights on.
I would call her name out like a chant,
repeating it with every exhalation,
soft in her ear at first, then loud, then louder,
as we fell backward over a high wall
into blankness.
                                It's stuff like that stays with you.
So, when her voice came to me over the line
in a phone booth in Cologne, near the cathedral,
the gist of it was like the crack of ice
constricting on a mountainside, and I
realized if I hung up the phone
that would be it.

There's someone outside waiting for the booth.
After five minutes in the ice and snow,
he starts banging on the door as if to say
when will you be done, I need the phone.
And I'm behind the glass, just hanging on,
and asking her how come she's back with him.
He's in the room. I think I almost hear him.
I know because she used to talk to him that way.
He'd call when I was there, and she'd pretend
I wasn't, which was cruel of her and sexy.
He's right there, and she's naked, on the edge
of the futon and it's nine o'clock in the morning.
And now the German guy starts hammering
his fist against the booth, so I just stop.

It's funny: I remember bits and pieces:
the caramel-colored duvet and the curl
her lip made when she smiled, her body leaning
above me, choking laughter hoarse with tears,
the way her eyes were like a little kid's.
I thought, that's it, you know?
                                                            I started reading
the Bible. I tore out the Old Testament
and carried it around. But you don't die.
You live for longer than you think you will.
Of course, there's things that won't let you forget
how what you wanted is what hurt you most,
how it was happiness itself betrayed you.

"Well, let's away and say how much is done."

III.
Snow was piling up knee-deep in Munich,
at least where we were staying in the cramped
side streets near the station — a Turkish slum.
And we were in a war.
                                                "Kein Blut für Öl"
was scrawled in red spray paint across the walls.
They didn't want us there. Nobody did.

                            "We are all Germans here,"
some radish-faced Bayerische drunkard yells
over the Beatles in the Café Americain—
that's right, the goddamned Café *Americain*.
He yells it at Macduff, an Irish guy,
(not Scots, but close enough for bus and truck).
We got a lot of that, both north and south.
So, here's the Black Forest. Here's the North Sea.

Let's say this squiggly line's the Autobahn,
and every day we'd drive at record speed
from Aachen to Stuttgart, Stuttgart to Freiberg,
Freiberg to Cologne, four towns a week.

Because I'm Malcolm, I get to be the king,
which I thought was pretty cool, except, get this,
my grand finale always got a laugh.
I'm up there heaving out my guts, and just
as I start to raise the crown above my head
with stage light pouring through this golden O
(a moment that you dream about in school)
— that's when the laughter starts.
And not just giggles.
No, no. A nervous laugh, like wildfire.
It wasn't my acting, though that was bad
enough — more lame than laughable, I'm sure.
They laughed because each night, right at the curtain,
they'd fly in a giant banner of my head
to replace the one they'd torn down of Macbeth.
The drops were painted by some kid in Queens,
With tempera paint or house paint, I don't know.
So, when they dropped the thing, each night we'd hear
this far-off rumble like an engine grinding.
This floor-to-ceiling banner of my face
was fucking cross eyed. You believe that shit?

Did you ever see Polanski's film of *Macbeth*?
It's got great stuff. But mostly that's because
Kenneth Tynan told him what was what.
That Banquo's children shall be kings, we know.
We also know that Malcolm's on the throne.
So, here's the thing.
Macbeth has got no kids, none that we know of.

But Lady's given suck, that's how she puts it,
so what is what? What happened to her kid?
(I know, I'm getting literal.) Behind the credits,
a figure in a cloak — who must be Banquo's son —
goes to see the witches. It never ends.
One thane betrays another, blood for blood,
blood for blood. And so on and on.
Sometimes it's hard to know how it began,
how what they wanted was the thing they wanted.
"What's to be done?"
                                        Days off we used for sightseeing:
end of the streetcar line, there is the fence,
then squares marking the places that they slept.
Behind is the iron door that kept the flames,
and overhead the sky where they saw the smoke.

The gate on which we read the words was here.
Behind the gate, the path bends to the left.
The crematorium is sort of here.

Half of us could easily have died there.
Half of us would have been the ones who lived.

IV.
I don't want to talk about it. Only . . .
change the subject, can we? Twenty years,
so long I can't remember who I was.
Though mostly I'm the same. I have the same
marks set down against me on the slate.
That's how I think of it sometimes, like marks,
like hatch marks on a perfect field of white.

The sun is setting in you, the snow is falling in you . . .

I hate this song. It's crap.
                                                  And mostly I
Don't think about it, really. Why do that?
I only get more miserable that way.
We'd talk at night. He'd call from Germany.
He was in a play. So, yeah, we'd talk.
Which was the worst, since months went by
that I couldn't tell him. I just couldn't.

Your face is like a mirror, your face inside my mirror …

I prayed, you know, that it might not be true:
the lateness. Then I'm ten or twelve weeks on,
and he's off god-knows-where, calling me up
on Sunday mornings. I think I kind of lost it.
Enough, I thought, enough, you know? I told him
I was back with my old boyfriend. That was it.
He never called me after that. Which scared me.

How can it be the same, if it was never that way?

It was just simpler on my own, and I
didn't want to know what he would say …
didn't want to hear him make that sound
like I should know exactly what to do.
I had no help, and I did what I did,
the only thing that at the time made sense.
A life ago. That's not me anymore.

It's just the tide of your eyes, washing away the shore.

You can hear the church bells from here. If you
wait a minute we can hear them now.
The bells are like the snow. They make things quiet.

And when they ring then everything around them
is quiet and the sound of quiet is
the sound between the rings, between the noise.
The same with snow, especially when it's new.

I love the snow, the way it wipes the street
clear for a little while, before the dogs,
before the plows make muddy hills of it,
before the road-salt and the sidewalk-salt
dissolves it into dirty lakes and streams.
For a second it is clean and blank and quiet.
It's a miracle, how muted it can be,

like all the sound's absorbed into itself.
I like to stand outside there, on the street,
without the traffic in the early morning
with a new snowfall blanketing the street,
only my breath like feathers in the cold.
That's when I talk to God — don't laugh at me —
and actually feel for sure he's listening.

This one time I was driving, New Year's Day.
I was driving to a friend's. The road was empty.
It was early, just me and the snow
on long slow curves between two mountain peaks:
a whiteout — road and trees and sky all white,
snow falling like a bed sheet on the hood.
Then, around the bend, a shadow in the road.

I didn't slow down. It was just a shadow.
But then, too late, I saw it was a deer
that had been run down by another car.
I wound up skidding halfway off the road.

When I got out, the place was a cathedral
with giant walls of white, even the deer
seemed pristine, a perfect antlered buck,

except for the halo of frozen blood
around its head. Its eyes were filled with snow,
I felt sick, kind of queasy, and I thought
that I should do something for this deer
like drag him to the shoulder, but I just
left him in that paradise of snow.
Was it the blood that made it seem so holy?

You bleed when you get a tattoo, don't you?
Sometimes I think of getting one. Today,
I woke up after dreaming that I had one,
in brilliant colors on a white background,
a streak of purple written into white,
on the slope of my back, all across my back,
indelible against a field of white.

V.

I met this girl in Freiberg after the run,
where someone had a car, and we piled in
for the Schwartzwald hairpin drive to Prague for Easter.
The fields were filled with Soviet concrete,
with rusted pylons and abandoned trains,
just drying out like carrion in the sun,
In one small town, I crapped into a hole
in the ground from which a board had been removed.
We stayed a couple days in a family flat
belonging to some Czech friends of the girl —
Greta? — who later let me in her sleeping bag.

But it was after, in her dorm, the others gone,
when we actually shared a bed. By now it's spring.

On the morning of the day that I was leaving,
we made love in the cold lattice of sunlight
that came in through her window. It was nice,
and I remember thinking that my girlfriend
could care less who I slept with. I was happy
that I had someone, that soon I'd be leaving.
I felt giddy. I felt wrung out and loved,
if only briefly. Though it wasn't love
I felt exactly — more like free of love.
I was glad when it was time to get away,
to Paris on the night-line sleeper train.

An oubliette—a train inside a tunnel.

"Was not that nobly done?"

I saw her one more time back in New York —
Sasha — and then again, I guess about a year ago,
six or seven months before she died.
It was a suicide. I should have told you that.
She seemed okay, you know? She seemed . . . the same.
We drank a fifth of Scotch out of the bottle.
I was so wasted out on Amsterdam,
feeling sick and walking toward the train,
with the cold coming on and early dusk.
Seems a long time ago.
"I gin to be aweary of the sun . . ."

Sunlight shone on her face inside the diner:
Is the body ever holy except in memory?

I learned
that I was capable of anything.

Christian Wiman (b. 1966)

From England, the late poet and polymath Clive James once wrote of Christian Wiman: "His rhymes and line-turnovers are all carefully placed to intensify the speech rhythms, making everything dramatic: not shoutingly so, but with a steady voice that tells an ideal story every time." Wiman planted a forty-one-page family narrative as the title poem of his first book, *The Long Home* (Copper Canyon Press, 1998), winner of the Nicolas Roerich Poetry Prize. *Hard Night* (Copper Canyon Press, 2005) was his next original collection, followed by *Every Riven Thing* (2011), *Once in the West* (2014), and *Survival Is a Style* (2020)—all published by Farrar, Straus and Giroux. In *Stolen Air* (Ecco, 2012), he translated the poems of Osip Mandelstam (1891–1938). He has also edited three anthologies: *Home: 100 Poems* (Yale University Press, 2021), *Joy: 100 Poems* (Yale University Press, 2017), and, with Don Share, *The Open Door* (University of Chicago Press, 2013), poems celebrating one hundred years of *Poetry*, where Wiman reigned as editor from 2003 to 2013.

"Poetry," he claimed in an April 2004 editorial for the magazine, "is predicated on the existence of an inner life." Three years later, in an essay for the *American Scholar*, he revealed that he had been diagnosed with an incurable blood cancer. Thereafter, his prose writings became increasingly contemplative, combining memoir with reflections on belief and the poetic vocation. Those books include *Ambition and Survival: Becoming a Poet* (Copper Canyon Press, 2004); *My Bright Abyss: Meditation of a Modern Believer* (Farrar, Straus and Giroux, 2013); *He Held Radical Light: The Art of Faith, the Faith of Art* (Farrar, Straus and Giroux, 2018); and *Zero at the Bone: Fifty Entries against Despair* (Farrar, Straus and Giroux, 2023).

Born in the town of Snyder in West Texas, Wiman graduated from Washington and Lee University. A former Guggenheim Fellow, he has taught at Stanford University, Northwestern University, Lynchburg College, the Prague School of Economics, and Yale Divinity School, where he is professor of the practice of religion and literature.

THE ICE STORM

Then all one day because of ice
they couldn't make it down the hill.
Or up, James says,
dabbing at a spill
of coffee, crunching toast as if it had a spine.
But he could work, at any rate,
could concentrate
on that book he's been reading,
or meaning to,
the flu—
or was it famine?—of '49,
some smoldering fact
he's found in the cold ash of some war.
Gusting upward, lobes and nose on fire,
his whole face florid
from the heart attack
he's somehow never had,
he sways, repeating:
Oh, we'd get down just fine,
I expect, but we'd never make it back,
then goes into his room and shuts the door.

Eva's hours have nearer ends.
She heats the little disk the cat sleeps on;
chips, until her hands are gone,
the glaze off all the feeders for the birds;
then writes two friends
to thank them for the birthday chocolates they've sent.
The word alone makes her stomach burn.
Which is mostly what age is, she's learned,
the senses sharpening backwards,

keen to what they can't perceive,
when to be wise means mostly not to wish
for what you love,
for what you love is pain:
spices or coffee, gin
bringing the evening light into your veins,
good chocolates the grandkids ravish
like a horde of crows.
You stuff your bellies with tomorrow's ache,
she can almost hear him bellow,
nipping and pinching to make them squeal.
Hot water with honey, one coddled egg, dry saltines:
Oh, what difference does it make?
She picks up the chocolates, breaks
the seal.

He draws the blinds on a wall of glass,
winces at the glare,
drags his chair
into the bright crevasse
between his bed and bookshelf,
takes a deep breath of air,
and buries himself
into one of the early wordy furies
of William Gladstone,
never a man for minor keys.
Creak and tick of the burdened limbs.
A creak and tick inside of him
as he crosses his legs and then uncrosses them,
shifts his weight to ease
the stiffness in one side,
turns a page like a summit he has climbed,

and breathes . . .
Think of it—twenty thousand books devoured
in Gladstone's life, and of his own
enough to keep an army of bibliographers occupied;
a whole age and empire crammed into one man:
spellbinding crowds until he couldn't stand,
felling his million trees,
filling six decades' worth of diaries
because a life is owed as well as owned, time
a gift of which a good man gives account;
who would mount,
night after night, a moral, high-rhetorical siege
upon some poor Haymarket tart
in whom ruin
and beauty were one word,
then go home and whip himself for a sin
that, all the evidence suggests, never occurred
but in his heart.

And has just one,
pleasure spreading through her blood like a single drop
of ink.
She scours the stove and countertop,
bleaches coffee stains off the sink,
cleans leaf by leaf
the emerald ripple and the paradise palm,
both mostly dormant now,
reaches high for the philodendron, huge since trained to climb,
and pauses,
remembering the calm
of constant motion that her mother was—

a beauty, men said, though it hardly seemed
a part of her, looking out of her own face
like someone on a train;
and remembering, too,
the child-high hedgerows
along the lane
behind their house on Paddox Close,
the slice of sky above
growing wider as she grew,
the little park with its central statue
(who was it of?),
which, last time she'd seen,
weather had worried
to a Swedish ivy sort of green.

Emma Clifton, Elizabeth Collins, P. Lightfoot—
even the names of those women are there
amid the parliamentary proceedings,
bulldog scholarship, affairs
of state.
He lifts his hand like a weight
to check his watch, little trembles traveling through his bones
into the air
as through plucked strings
a sound.
Two hours until the final round
at Palm Springs,
with its hairpin fairways, lacquered greens,
and that great eighteenth in homage
to Bobby Jones.

What a character!—touring in his teens,
retired at twenty-eight
with nothing left to win,
at forty storming Normandy with men
half his age.
Even his death was rare—
syringomyelia—cane to brace to wheelchair
without a trace of self-pity, regret, rage:
We all have to play the ball as it lies.
How much of a man's revealed in how he dies ...
Poor Owen, barely sixty, Dean of the College,
a decent book on Kant behind him:
two days of chest pain
slivering into a lifetime's knowledge
and all the old beliefs
come flooding back,
silly relics and rituals, griefs
you're born into, some guilt you can't even name.
"Ischemia," that's exactly right: blood lack.

Sweet pickles and white bread,
salted ham,
a soybean spread
that is his one concession to his heart,
two butter cookies, plum jam:
she clicks
across the polished floor
through motes that rise
and float like molecules of light,
pausing outside his door,
hearing the Mahler chorus to which he always cries,
plays *to* cry, she suspects,
as if even sadness could be planned.

She takes the knob in her hand,
sees, inside its shine,
white tablecloths, crystal cut fine
as jewels,
and, and . . . and a man
with American shoulders and vowels,
that face
so open it wasn't, like the ocean,
and that tidal way he had of filling any space
that wasn't taken,
the table where he sat with friends,
afternoons and weekends,
classrooms, boardrooms, lecture halls,
the very bodies of their children,
in whose broad limbs he seems to sprawl.
Was that what she had fallen for,
talk of golf, and Oxford, and roast beef
in that gray decade after the war,
that it seemed so safe
a fall?

There—where the strings go silent
and that woman's whole soul
is in his throat . . .
A home can have but one composer.
Wasn't that the quote?
That long ironclad letter Mahler wrote
to Alma, the most exquisite
woman in Vienna, who packed
away that cold contract,
her party dresses, and her own precocious technique,
and settled, if you could call it that,

into the role
of being Gustav Mahler's wife:
I am not happy, yet not unhappy.
My ship is in the harbor, but it has sprung a leak.
But he *loved* her; and she is in his music
as surely as the God
he never quite possessed nor fully lost,
as surely as the daughter is alive
inside this song, whose life
it cost.
Gladstone also had a daughter die at five.
Odd,
not to have thought of that before.
And Mahler's sister's name was Anna,
and Gladstone's sister Ann;
and wasn't Gladstone's family from Oxford, or near?
Oh, William dear,
she told him once, *if you weren't such a great man,*
you'd be a terrible bore.

Was that a laugh or a sob?
Mahler dies off
into the long silences, polite applause,
and weirdly reverential tones of golf.
This could take all day.
She lets go of the knob,
backs away.

He looks up as if he's heard a sound—
what was it called,

that late-medieval game out of which golf evolved?
He looks down:
O'Connor's on the second tee.
It must have started earlier than he thought.
Steady head, steady head,
that pro at Sea Pines always said.
James lifts one hand above his knee,
so palsied now
he can't keep his cocktails quiet,
as if every instant were a shock
his body took.
Think of a stake
driven through your skull into the ground.
California fades into some salesman fool
he mutes
to spend three minutes
amid the doomed midcentury debates
on Home Rule:
Gladstone, suicidally brilliant at eighty-four—
One fight more,
the best and the last . . .
He looks up to see a ball
that's made of feathers struck
with something like a gardening tool
and flying fast
toward what, in the moment before he blinks,
is a cemetery gate.
Hurley or *shinty*, he thinks
as it falls.
In northern France they called it *soule*.

Head bowed,
her face in pieces
on the table, she seems,
as she gathers and releases
a little storm of gleams
from her hands, to wield the sun she's in.
Nineteen fifty-four it would have been
when James's parents gave them these. Proud,
so proud they were—
of their heirloom silver, their tidy house, Michigan,
her,
whom they kept introducing as James's bride,
though she was nearly five months gone by then.
She draws the cloth between the light and knife,
freezes.
How strange—to feel a life
that is and isn't yours
shift inside.
After the first brittle exchanges that day,
hot dogs and crisps, tours
of their property, their church, James's high school
where they first learned their private awe was real,
his mother rattling on in that white-noise way
that women will
when silence, like men,
is simply one more thing to fill—
Eva had nodded, and smiled,
and hovered just outside of her own skin,
trying to feel
that life inside of her again.

The dogleg seventh. A tough par five,
the fairway pared
to nearly nothing at its kink,
ramping up to inkblot bunkers and a pulpit green.
O'Connor times a drive
so pure and powerful the ball becomes the air—
a blue nowhere
for a long moment on the screen—
distilling white on its descent
into the rough.
Straight enough,
the commentator says, *but overplayed,*
going on to praise the progress O'Connor's made
since that wild tirade
two years ago on this same course,
the midnight tabloid accident
in which he broke both hands.
The camera pans
the fairway and milling gallery,
probes a dense, occluded spot
under a tree.
As if a man could simply start all over,
as if you couldn't read one character
in everything he does.
What was it Mahler said of Alma's early love—
Even his music has a weak chin.
O'Connor, lost in leaves, eye on the pin,
scalds a shot
past every limb but one,
which, after a comic chaos
of ricochets,
trickles back exactly where it was.
The Perilous Ambition
was Bobby Jones's phrase,

which is to aim at what you were
despite the hazard you are in.

Anna calls,
the fifth time in as many days,
some childhood memory of a sauce
for pears;
thirty minutes later calls again
to chat about the ice
she's seen on television,
one brother's ruined marriage,
another's move across
the country, cutting a careful trace
around the silence
of her second miscarriage
in as many years
until there is no word that's not that loss.
A walk, I think. You too, Mom. Tell Dad hi.
Goodbye.

This stiffness in one side,
the telephone ringing and ringing,
the damn birds racketing
as if it were spring—
he's up, listing a moment while the tide
of blood comes back into his brain,
a fine pain
needling through his chest and down one shoulder,
which is what he should have told her,
he thinks, with as much a smile

as he can manage, that pretty girl he stumbled into in the aisle
of the grocery store,
who had pink-streaked hair, a pierced nose, and swore
by acupuncture:
that his body had, in a sense, acquired its own.
Point by point he feels the pain withdraw.
Like a world disturbed in water,
his bed and bookcase, the centuries on the shelves,
the television, and his own unsteady limbs
waver back into themselves.
Gladstone,
he thinks, striding across the room,
that mix of filial relief and Protestant rage
the great man felt for his sister, healed of lockjaw
and tremblings by the knucklebone
of a saint.
He stops, so close that he can see
each nub and flaw
in the white paint
of the door.
He takes a deep breath, lets it out slowly.
What's one hour more.

Forks and spoons and knives.
Fingers, hair, face.
What survives,
she wonders, rising suddenly toward the window,
of James's parents' place:
the vegetable garden and the screened-in porch,
the driveway bumping toward
the blacktop, as they called it,

splintering into a million little nameless roads
through the countryside
that she and James didn't so much drive
one frozen night not so long ago
as glide.
She puts her fingers on the cold pane:
the iron deck chairs, the railings and the ground below,
each least tip of every tree,
all wrought to the same fine fragility
of glass.
Where were they?
She feels a quicksilver current in her nerves,
feels it pass.
Was there some way
to have prepared for this—
the childhood walks; the first lilt and flirt
of a voice she hardly recognized as hers;
that kiss
outside her front door
after James had met her parents, the taste
of something, tea, yes;
and more,
Amherst, New Haven, Ann Arbor,
vast tracts of life like landscape glimpsed from a car;
even labor,
Lord, vise of time
tightening, tightening, tearing you in two
until that one pain is all you are . . .
—these brief gleams in the mind.
And who would guess
that as the years find
their final focus you're bothered less
by the dark that lies ahead of you
than the dark that lies behind?

But who'd refuse a healing for its source?
Up, up
the slick eighteenth a strong putt climbs,
rounds
the lip of the cup
so deeply half the ball's inside,
emerges
only to slide
all the way back down.
Tough course, tough course.

North, night, late, and the branches fraught
with ice as they are now;
first one owl
like an oboe in the upper dark,
low, stark,
then farther off another;
and how,
as the time between their cries grew wide,
they never moved,
as if what each one sought
was not the other
but the distance that the other was,
and cried
but to align their silences.

He lifts his eyes:
a last stab of light from the icy trees.
Tomorrow this will all be gone.
The limbs will unclench, the ground give,
and the melt
from the branchtip and rooftop tick, tick all day long
like a rain.
Why did you suffer? Why did you live?
Things fever out of their forms again,
and he sees, blurred
into the list of names on the screen,
the first golfer of whom there's record,
King James of the Iron Belt,
who died in arms on the fields of Flodden.
Live long enough and all thoughts go one way—
Gladstone, cancer hiving his face,
turning on that last railway platform to say:
God bless you all, and this place,
and the land you love;
Mahler, harrowed and honed by the fever
he'd soon die of:
I am hungrier for life than ever.
Even this muted Midwestern woman
purging germs
on TV brings his mother back,
her eyes emptying, her chest ripped apart
by doctors frantically massaging that starved heart,
which feels, he's read somewhere, like a seethe of worms.

Let it go.
Let the silver lie scattered as it is,
dinner unprepared.

Let an hour go by in glimpses
of the old oak iced in light like a chandelier,
titmouse and sparrow,
a cardinal like a cut the tree releases
calling *what-cheer, cheer, cheer.*
What is the cry she can't recognize?
What time is it now,
a prow
of last light slicing through the deep shadow
of the living room where she lies,
opera on public radio,
while the cat purrs
into the warm crook of limbs it's found,
and the deep-water heartbeat sound inside of sound
is hers,
the kiss still on her lips
as she slips
inside after the last goodbyes,
where her long-dead father from behind his paper mutters
You can bet they call him Jim,
And her mother, later, even quieter,
Do you love him?

Let it go.
Let the dead recede
into their names,
effect lie quiet with its cause.
In the end,
what difference does it make,
another day in grains,
walls a gauze

through which fine, faint voices bleed.
It will all come clear tomorrow.
Let the ache
that feels like acid rising in his chest
as he lies down on his bed to rest
from what it seems he's just begun
be only that.
Let it be done,
if not for good then for now,
if for good then with grace somehow,
the screen
flickering with whatever victory or defeat
one can always read about,
evening intensifying inside and out
until there is no pane between,
his eyes becoming heavy, and all he knows
grown light,
as he lets them—*Eva?*—close.

Rachel Wetzsteon (1967–2009)

Rachel Wetzsteon's first book, *The Other Stars* (Penguin, 1994), was chosen by John Hollander (1929–2013) for the National Poetry Series. In her brief life, she published two other poetry books—*Home and Away* (Penguin, 1998) and *Sakura Park* (Persea, 2006)—and *Influential Ghosts* (Routledge, 2007), an academic study of W. H. Auden. In late December 2009, she died by suicide. A posthumous collection, *Silver Roses* (Persea), was issued the following year.

In many of her poems, notably in *Sakura Park*, this Manhattan native hymned the Upper West Side neighborhood of Morningside Heights. She earned a bachelor's degree from Yale University, a master's from Johns Hopkins University, and a PhD from Columbia University. Honors included the American Academy of Arts and Letters' Witter Bynner Prize for Poetry and an Ingram Merrill Foundation grant. Wetzsteon was on the faculty of William Patterson University in New Jersey, taught at the Unterberg Poetry Center of the 92nd Street Y, and served briefly as poetry editor for the *New Republic*.

Formal finesse, characteristic humor, and a love for classic Hollywood films are observed in this poem, a pantoum. It adapts scenes from Alfred Hitchcock's 1958 masterpiece, featuring Jimmy Stewart and Kim Novak.

MADELEINE FOR A WHILE

after Hitchcock's Vertigo

Scottie looked down from a very great height,
and as Midge sat primly at her easel
he talked himself back into wholeness:
"I look up, I look down, I look up, I look . . ."

As Midge sat primly at her easel
he followed Madeleine through the city.
"I look up, I look down, I look up, I look . . ."
Down he fell all over again.

He followed Madeleine through the city;
the ghost of mad Carlotta steered her.
Down he fell all over again:
she jumped in the water and he jumped after.

The ghost of mad Carlotta steered her:
"There's someone within me, and she says I must die."
She jumped in the water and he jumped after;
they kissed in the shade of ancient sequoias.

"There's someone within me, and she says I must die."
Haunted Madeleine mounted the steps.
They kissed in the shade of ancient sequoias,
they parted when she leaped from the tower.

Haunted Madeleine mounted the steps;
Scottie pursued, obsessed and dizzy.
They parted when she leaped from the tower,
they met again in a crowded rush hour.

Scottie pursued, obsessed and dizzy.
An ill-lit corridor led to her room.
They met again in a crowded rush hour;
They argued in her fleabag hotel.

An ill-lit corridor led to her room;
Judy's dark hair confused the picture.
They argued in her fleabag hotel.
"Be Madeleine for a while," he begged.

Judy's dark hair confused the picture,
ruining the marvelous story.
"Be Madeleine for a while," he begged,
so she returned a dazzling blonde.

Ruining the marvelous story,
her necklace revealed all she had been
when she returned a dazzling blonde.
Holding Madeleine, he'd embraced air.

Her necklace revealed all she had been:
a stumble, a wail, a plunge into darkness.
Holding Madeleine, he'd embraced air.
One final thing and he would be free.

A stumble, a wail, a plunge into darkness.
He talked himself back into wholeness:
one final thing and he would be free.
Scottie looked down from a very great height.

A. E. Stallings (b. 1968)

In 2023, Alicia Elisbeth Stallings became Oxford University's professor of poetry, an elected office created in 1708. She was born in Decatur, Georgia, earned an AB in classics from the University of Georgia and a master of studies (MSt) in Latin literature from Oxford (Lady Margaret Hall). While still in high school, she published poems in paying venues such as *Seventeen* magazine. Her first book, *Archaic Smile* (University of Evansville Press, 1999), won the Richard Wilbur Award; her second, *Hapax* (TriQuarterly Books, 2006), the Poets' Prize. *Olives* (TriQuarterly Books, 2012) was a finalist for the National Book Critics Circle Award. In 2018, Farrar, Straus and Giroux brought out *Like*, a finalist for the Pulitzer Prize in Poetry. *The Afterlife: Selected Poems* (Farrar, Straus and Giroux) appeared in 2022.

Stallings is a classicist in both senses of the word: acute observations about nature, travel, and family or social relations are rendered in rhyme and meter, while references to antiquity abound. Her book-length translations include Lucretius's *The Nature of Things* (2009) and Hesiod's *Work and Days* (2019)—both published by Penguin Classics—and *The Battle between the Frogs and Mice* (Paul Dry Books, 2019), an ancient Greek fable. She is a member of the American Academy of Arts and Sciences and has received fellowships from the MacArthur Foundation, the Guggenheim Foundation, and the National Endowment for the Arts. A resident of Athens, Greece, Stallings has taught at summer poetry workshops there and in the United States. She frequently publishes prose in the *London Review of Books*, the *Times Literary Supplement*, and other literary periodicals. In the spring of 2023, the *Hudson Review* ran her essays on how artists historically have "framed the ongoing debate" about ownership of the Elgin Marbles.

"Battle of Plataea: Aftermath" is a retelling of vignettes from Herodotus's (484–425 BC) history of the Greco-Persian wars. The Battle of Plataea, like the concurrent Battle of Mycale, marked a decisive victory for the Greeks. In this narrative poem, as if in deference to Herodotus, Stallings recasts a sonnet sequence into prose. The other entry here, "Lost and Found," applies the verse form *ottava rima*.

BATTLE OF PLATAEA: AFTERMATH

Out of Book Nine of the Histories of Herodotus

THE SPARTAN GENERALS

After the blood-brimmed field, we were amazed to stride
into those empty silken tents—bright tapestries, wrought
silver ornaments, the furnishings of solid gold. Eyes glazed
at all the untold booty: gods be praised! Our king bid for-
eign cooks spare no expense to make the meal our foes
would eat, prepare their pastries, spices, wine. Such slowly
braised flesh melting off the bone! Such colors, scents! Our
king laughed as he laid out on the cloth, beside the feast,
our ration of the black broth: "Behold! They came to rob us of
our fare!" We also laughed, though fed up with that food,
the soldier's mess, the black broth of blood.

THE CONCUBINES

We heard the Greeks had won. At once I went and decked
myself with every bracelet, ring, gold necklace that I
owned, and rouged my cheeks, and hastily had my maids
arrange my hair. The other concubines slumped in de-
spair; but I'd been snatched from Kos; my people, Greeks!
Dressed in white robes of silk, we fled the tent, and drove
through corpses, far as the eye could see, until I saw Pau-
sanias, the king. I stepped with golden sandals through the
gore, the lady that I was, and not the whore, and knelt, a

supplicant, *Please set me free.* The roar of blood like silence in my ear, until: "Lady, arise, be of good cheer."

LAMPON THE AEGINITE

"Your glory after this victory is sealed," I told Pausanias, to please him. "Now crown it with revenge for Leonidas beheaded at Thermopylae. Remember the restitution that Xerxes denied us, and how he said Mardonius would pay it? Well, here is the cadaver—you just say it—and we'll impale Mardonius's head." He stood in silence as his face went somber. "Stranger," he addressed me, "on this field the crime was well avenged." As for that corpse, who knows what happened to it? There are versions—the truth is not so straight it never warps. Someone interred it—so I've heard it said—and reaped a handsome bounty from the Persians.

THE IMMORTALS

He called us the Immortals—the select companions who would battle at his side, Mardonius on his white charger. Pride, we felt, of course; maybe we half believed we were that day, not helmeted or greaved, no golden scales under the robes we wore. We wielded wicker shields for catching arrows. We were surrounded, as on mountain hunts a pack of Spartan hounds surrounds the boar. In that tight space, we knew our hopes were wrecked, like ships, frail bridges over Hellesponts, the horsewhipped waters bridling at the narrows. We were caught up in doom, as fish or sparrows, grateful like other men to die but once.

ARISTODEMUS THE COWARD

I lie here without honor, as I willed. Alone among those at Thermopylae I lived—if it is life to loathe each breath. They say I was the bravest Spartan here, but that I broke formation, and I fought not only as one not afraid of death, but one who seeks it, battle-mad, distraught. A Spartan soldier never leaves the line. It took so many Persians to get killed, I slogged on, drunk with slaughter as with wine. And when at last I met the foeman's spear, I laid my body down like shame, now free to fall amidst the dust, having fulfilled the ranks of the two hundred and ninety-nine.

LOST AND FOUND

I.

I crawled all morning on my hands and knees
Searching for what was lost—beneath a chair,
Behind the out-of-tune piano. *Please*,
I prayed to Entropy, let it be there—
Some vital Lego brick or puzzle piece
(A child bereft is hiccoughing despair),
A ball, a doll's leg popped out of its socket,
Or treasures fallen through a holey pocket.

II.

Amazing what webbed shadows can conceal—
A three-wheeled Matchbox car, or half a brace
Of socks or shoes. Oblivion will steal
Promiscuously—lost without a trace,
Microscopic bits of Playmobil,
The backup set of house keys. You misplace
Your temper and your wits, till you can exhaust
All patience with the hours it has cost.

III.

I thought too of that parable, the other—
Not the one men preach of the lost sheep,
The lesser-known one, on the housewife's bother
Over a missing coin: how she must sweep
The house to find it. No doubt, *she* was a mother,
I think, and laugh, and then I want to weep:
The hours drained as women rearrange
The furniture in search of small, lost change.

IV.

"Tidy up your room," I told my son,
"That way, it's easier to look." (It's true.)
He made an effort, a halfhearted one
Abandoned after just a block or two.
"It isn't fair," he said, "it isn't fun,
I never do what *I* would like to do,
But you, you always do *just what you want.*"
Which plucked a string, as though a cosmic taunt.

V.

I paused. "Is *that* what you think, then," I said.
(Sometimes he seemed less seven-year-old boy
Than teenager.) "That making you go to bed
Or washing dishes is something I *enjoy*,
And that I've nothing better to do instead
Of hunting for a crappy plastic toy?"
Raised voices, tears, apologies all round,
And yet the crucial piece was never found.

VI.

That night I was still seeking in my dreams,
Still groping after fragments and the maimed,
Just as in dreams a seamstress stitches seams,
Or politician spins truth unashamed,
Or, loping through remembered fields and streams,
The hound pursues the scent that can't be named,
Her paws a-twitch, though heavily she lies,
And dogsbody the body does not rise,

VII.

Or as a poet stalks a skittish rhyme
Behind her lidded eyes, beneath the mask
Of sleep—because the mind has no free time
But keeps at night to its diurnal task
And pushes the stone as high as it can climb
Before it trochees down again, Don't ask
The mind to rest, though someday it must cease;
In life, only the flesh has any peace.

VIII.

It seemed I searched, though, in a dusty place
Beneath a black sky thrilled with stars, ground strewn
With stones whose blotting shade seemed to erase
The land's gleam (like a tarnished silver spoon);
A figure neared, with adumbrated face,
Who said, "This is the valley on the moon
Where everything misplaced on earth accrues,
And here all things are gathered that you lose."

IX.

The moon? Yet I did not dispute the claim.
She seemed familiar—hard to tell among
Such alien surroundings. All the same,
A word seemed out of reach, tip of my tongue,
Close-clustered consonants and vowels, a name.
Beneath her hood I glimpsed a face not young
But elegant, refined as it grew older.
My name she knew, although I hadn't told her.

X.

Now that my eyes had focused in the dark
I saw that what seemed mountains, ridges, hills
All hemmed around us, flinging down their stark
Chill silhouettes, were overflowing landfills,
Huge heaps of congeries. And I could mark
The mounds of keys or orphaned socks, dropped pills
(Those were the things that I could recognize),
Like bombed-out cities black against the skies.

XI.

Somehow it brought to mind the vestibule
Jumbled with hats, umbrellas, backpacks, totes,
Scarves, gym shoes, that they keep at my son's school
Behind the lunchroom: bins of winter coats,
Hairbands, sunglasses stacked up on a stool—
Each thing spoke volumes or quipped anecdotes—
Lorn, makeless gloves; lunch boxes starting to mottle.
(I'd come to seek an AWOL water bottle.)

XII.

"Look there," she said, and gestured to the keys,
"Those are the halls to which we can't return—
The rooms where we once sat on others' knees,
Grandparents' houses, loving, spare, and stern,
Tree houses where we whispered to the trees
Gauche secrets, virgin bedrooms where we'd burn,
Love's first apartments. As we shut each door,
It locks: we cannot enter anymore."

XIII.

There was a mound that loomed above our heads,
A skein of dusty strands large as a barn.
"Are these," I asked, "the sins of hair one sheds
In life, or all the rips one has to darn?"
She laughed and said, "These are the frayed, lost threads
Of conversations, arguments, the yarn
Of thought and logic's clews we'd thought we'd spun
Only to find they'd somehow come undone."

XIV.

Then there was sunk, among the hills, a bowl,
A wide, shallow depression, in which "O"s
Or ciphers gathered, thin, and black as coal,
Like washers of black iron. I asked, "And those?"
"They mark our absences—it's through the hole
Of lapsed attention that the moment goes."
I thought of those assemblies with repentance
Where I had mocked the prizes of attendance.

XV.

"And that?" I gestured to a pyramid
Of papers, ever threatening to tumble.
It shifted—sheaves of pages suddenly slid
Then seemed to settle. I stepped back from the jumble,
Thinking we might be buried there amid
An avalanche of foolscap. A hushed rumble
Shuffled its menace. I whispered, "Then are those
The poems lost, or pages of sure prose—

XVI.

"Maybe even something that would sell
(A book about a young aspiring warlock?)—
That disappeared when something broke the spell,
When toddler learned to work the study door-lock,
Or telephone brayed bad news—or the front bell
Portended importunity from Porlock?"
"The poems," she said, "that perish at the brink
Of being, aren't so many as you think,

XVII.

"Nor yet as great. No, no, those are the letters
We meant to write and didn't—all the unsaid
Begrudged congratulations to our betters,
Condolences we owed the lately dead,
Love notes unsent—in love, we all are debtors—
Gratitude to teachers who penned in red
Corrections to our ignorant defenses,
Apologies kept close like confidences."

XVIII.

A vague, headachy cloud among the towers
Rose, as heaps of gray down from black swans.
"Those are," she said, "Insomnia's desperate hours,
Lost sleep: countdown of clocks, the impotent yawns;
The teething cries, sweet drowsiness that sours,
The night feedings that soldier into dawns."
I watched as creatures, etiolated, pale,
Weighed bales of feathers in a brazen scale.

XIX.

What were the creatures doing? She explained,
"For every hour that we lose of sleep,
Another hour of wakefulness is gained;
There is a tally that we have to keep."
"Unbearable minutes!" She saw that I was pained.
"Perhaps," she said, "but sometimes in the deep
Of night, reflections come we cannot parse—
To *consider* means to contemplate the stars."

XX.

Skittering round us, skirls of silver sand
Would swarm and arch into a ridge or dune,
And then disperse, as if an unseen hand
Swept them away (there was no wind), then soon
Accumulate elsewhere, a sarabande
Of form and entropy, a restive swoon
Of particles, forever in a welter,
Like starling murmurations seeking shelter.

XXI.

"The sands of Time." (I didn't have to speak;
She answered straightaway with some disdain.)
"With scything hands you hasten through the week
Clockwise, while widdershins, the fair hours drain.
Haste," she declared, "is Violence, in Greek."
Then she bore on in silence once again.
"Why won't they rest?" I asked in puzzlement.
"Minutes are not lost," she said, "but spent."

XXII.

Nearby, a glint of vitreous splinters, foiled
With silver, bristled in a jagged mass.
"This is a woman's loveliness that's spoiled
With age," she said, "and tears, and days that pass—
Her raiment that is creased, thread-worn, and soiled.
Here, seek that vanished beauty in this glass."
And gave me a reflection where I sought her—
Nothing at first—but then I saw my daughter—

XXIII.

Eyes brown, not blue; the hair, not straight, but curled.
"Not truly lost," she laughed, at my surprise.
"Some things fetch up on the bright shores of the world
Once more, under a slightly different guise;
Meanwhile, they are not lost, but somehow furled
Back in the heart of things from which they rise."
And saying this, she turned, and did not wait,
But something nearby made me hesitate,

XXIV.

I couldn't make it out at first: a pile
Of bone chips, ivory splinters? Like a sleuth,
I sneaked a handful, following the while,
But stopped short when I realized the truth,
And let them fall, and dropped my neutral smile:
Each keen point was a tiny human tooth.
I looked back over my shoulder for a glimpse
And gasped to see a thousand, small grey imps

XXV.

Go scampering up the hill, with wrinkled wings
Leathern like bats, with backs hunched up to carry,
Slung on their shoulders, sacks bulged with grim things—
More teeth, I thought—remains you ought to bury.
My guide observed me watch their scurryings.
"But don't you recognize a real tooth fairy?
Each baby tooth, deciduous but bright,
Stands for a childhood rooted in delight,

XXVI.

"But those that come here stained, starting to rot,
Are childhoods that are eaten up with sorrow,
Eroded by the acids of their lot,
And others' sins they are compelled to borrow."
"So many!" I exclaimed, as fairies brought
More chatterings of teeth. "Yes, and tomorrow,
It never stops. Each childhood is outgrown
By sharper permanence. Even your own"

XXVII.

(Children, she meant) "cannot stay as they are.
Already, your son's childhood is consigned"—
She held up six fine milk teeth in a jar—
"Already he is leaving it behind,
Striding forth as light strides from a star;
And though the star blow out, inert and blind,
The light strides on, and reaches other eyes
That in some distant time scan these same skies."

XXVIII.

At last our path came to a spring whose gleam
Provoked my thirst. Two cups of battered zinc
Hung from a pair of books there: one had "Dream"
Inscribed upon it; on the other, "Think."
But when I dipped each cup's lip to the stream,
Immediately it began to sink.
When both had vanished, she said, "Do not wet
Your lips here with the waters of Forget."

XXIX.

Not water, though, I knew as I drew near it—
It was a liquid, true, but more like gin
Though smelling of aniseed—some cold, clear spirit
Water turns cloudy. "Many are taken in,
Some poets seek it, thinking that they fear it,
The reflectionless fountain of Oblivion.
By sex, by pills, by leap of doubt, by gas,
Or at the bottom of a tilting glass.

XXX.

"But you, you must remember, and return,"
Now I saw clearly skin of alabaster,
Her moon-washed hair, a gaze one could discern
As gunmetal grey—and then at last I asked her,
"Who are you? Are you She who used to burn
With sweetbitter eros? Or She who learned to master
The art of losing? She who did dying well,
Beekeeper's waspish daughter? Amherst's belle?"

XXXI.

"Don't you know? But everyone who loses
Has prayed and laid an offering at my shrine—
Though each who knows me calls me as she chooses,
My name's Mnemosyne; I am divine.
I am," she said, "the Mother of the Muses—
Imagine, you have two, but I have nine!
More even than that—for all the arts that be,
Sciences too, are born of Memory."

XXXII.

It made me smile, to think of her at her loom,
A gaggle of teenaged daughters at her feet:
No-nonsense Clio, Melpomene gothed in gloom,
Graceful Euterpe, Terpsichore, who won't eat,
Polyhymnia, with incense for perfume,
Thalia, laughing, Urania taking a seat
At the telescope, Erato fine-tuning her fiddle,
Calliope starting her story in the middle.

XXXIII.

She led the way now through a garden of musks
From dark, fanged flowers—incarnadine, maroon.
We came upon two gates: one made of tusks
Of prehistoric elephants, one hewn
From massive, savage horns. All round, the husks
And bones of great extinctions had been strewn.
"Here we must pass," she said, "but not together.
You pass through one; I shall go through the other."

XXXIV.

Then something began to happen. I felt her arm
On mine, we seemed to travel, standing still,
I saw a light. Had someone come to harm?
I heard a distant siren, pulsing, shrill—
But then I recognized the old alarm
Harping on its monitory trill—
It's Dawn again, come with her golden rule
Like a shepherd's crook, to harry us to school.

XXXV.

There are lunches to make, I thought, and tried to find
Some paperwork form last week I'd mislaid
(Due back, no doubt, today, dated and signed),
Instead, unearthed a bill we hadn't paid,
Located shoes, a scarf, a change of mind:
I tried to put aside mistakes I'd made,
To live in the sublunary, the swift,
Deep present, through which falling bodies sift.

XXXVI.

I saw the aorist moment as it went—
The light on my children's hair, my face in the glass
Neither old nor young; but bare, intelligent.
I was a sieve—I felt the moment pass
Right through me, currency as it was spent,
That bright, loose change, like falling leaves, that mass
Of decadent gold leaf, now turning brown—
I could not keep it; I could write it down.

Joshua Mehigan (b. 1969)

Joshua Mehigan's two full-length poetry books garnered critical acclaim upon publication, ten years apart. *The Optimist* (Ohio University Press, 2004) won the Hollis Summers Poetry Prize and was nominated for a *Los Angeles Times Book Review* Prize in Poetry. *Accepting the Disaster* found a commercial publisher in Farrar, Straus and Giroux, and earned citations in both the *Times Literary Supplement* and the *New York Times Book Review* as a best book of the year. Other laurels include fellowships from the Guggenheim Foundation and the National Endowment for the Arts, and the Levinson Prize from the Poetry Foundation. His poems have been rendered into German by Christophe Fricker.

Born in Johnstown, New York, Mehigan graduated from Purchase College and got an MFA from Sarah Lawrence College. He worked in communications and then taught, among other places, at various colleges in the City University of New York system. From 2017 to 2020, he was an Artist in Residence at Northwestern University. "The Orange Bottle" originally appeared in *Poetry* magazine, where Mehigan has also published prose, including "I Thought You Were a Poet" (July/August 2011 issue), a searching and often hilarious essay about his own experiences with mental disorders, and how they relate to poetry composition. For this piece, the Poetry Foundation awarded him an Editors Prize.

THE PIG ROAST

The afternoon wound down. The pool was calm.
Some children played around the emptied trough.
The small, low town was far enough away
behind the trees to look as though it were
a thread of road, some boxes, a toy steeple
propped on a branch. The parents bustled in
to cocktails when the lightning bugs began.
The children had the country on their shoes.
Outside, they watched the greasy farmhand set
a tractor's broken axle in the half-light.
They trailed him with a hundred aimless questions
until an aunt corralled them in the house.
A wobbly mother volunteered to fight
the crusted shoes and knotted laces off.
Outside, the farmhand closed his day. He crouched
beside the rifle hanging from the fence
and scratched the pig's broad head, then slowly rose
as though he'd left a teacup balanced there.
After the shot, the farmhand turned to spit,
and, with a rag, wiped from his dirty hands
what must have been the day, being done with it,
and turned then to the night, and night's demands.

THE DREAM JOB

He slid the new flights on and lined them up
and tacked them on and started welding them.
He went to take a leak and came right back
and then he slid the collar on the barrel
and set the indicator on the collar.
He rolled the barrel twice and got the reading,
six thousandths out, then marked it with the soapstone.
He stuck the ram in underneath and pumped,
then let it sit, then turned the knob. It settled.
He clocked out, showered, and drove the hour back home,
then kissed his son, then kissed his wife, then sat.
He ate his cube steak and drank his milk.
He watched the news and then whatever followed.
Then it was bed. He lay there in the dark
and smoked a cigarette. He kissed his wife
and closed his eyes and sank and got the reading,
three thousandths out. He pumped it up again,
a thousandth over, then backed off the knob.
It settled. That was done. He got the torch
and cut the flights, and got the hardface out,
hardfaced it, checked it over for low spots,
then, finally, sent it up to Harold. Then
they brought another. Then he woke for work.

THE ORANGE BOTTLE

The clear orange bottle was empty.
It had been empty a day.
It suddenly seemed so costly
and uncalled-for anyway.

Two years had passed. They had passed
more or less the way years should.
Maybe he'd changed. Or maybe
the doctors had misunderstood.

It was June. The enormous elm tree
was green again, and the scent
of hyacinth reached through the window
and followed wherever he went.

And the sky was the firmament!
His life was never better.
Each small white spotless cloud that passed
was like a long-wished-for letter.

But then he remembered his promise.
It came like a mild cramp,
and it sat there all day in the back of his mind
like a gas bill awaiting a stamp.

He saw three faces that Sunday,
mother, sister, niece,
all with the same kind, brown, scared eyes
that brought him no peace.

The sidewalk sparrows were peeping.
His whole house smelled like a flower.
But he remembered his promise.
The drugstore said one hour.

Back home again, he was tired.
The label said caution, said warning.
He left the clear orange bottle
on the lip of the sink till morning.

The insert said warning, said caution.
The insert said constipation.
It said insomnia, vivid dreams,
and hypersalivation,
  and increased urination,
  and a spinning sensation.

It also said night sweats, and
agranulocytosis,
and strongly suggested a full glass of water
be drunk with all doses.

The insert said all this,
the insert he never read.
But he didn't have to read it
to know what it said.

The bedroom was calm with moonlight
and the breeze through the screen was cooling.
Through the elm leaves the shivery light on the wall
came like quicksilver pooling.

But just before five, something woke him—
a close whisper—or maybe a far cry—
and the bedroom was queasy with light the color
of lapis lazuli.

He lay there listening hard
till six, till seven, till eight . . .
At nine he remembered his bottle.
But nine, nine was too late.

"Don't take me!" cried the clozapine.
"Don't take me!" cried the pill.
By ten he was feeling restless,
with a whole day left to kill.

"Don't take me!" cried the clozapine.
"Yes, don't!" cried the medication.
And the bright yellow morning seemed suddenly edged
with a shady fascination.

Why should he go to his workplace?
Who was his supervisor?
He had a snickering feeling
that he was becoming wiser.

His room filled up with interest.
He had begun to think!
He thought of the knives in the kitchen
and the bottles under the sink.

He thought as he switched the stove on
or stood at his shaving mirror,
or reached for his belt in the wardrobe.
Thinking made things clearer.

Even the bedroom window,
the open window full of sun,
continually hinted
at something that should be done.

But he was crooked and useless.
He was a piece of shit.
And so, as everyone knew he would,
he failed to go through with it.

"Don't take me!" cried the clozapine.
"Don't take me!" cried the drug.
Just then, the telephone rang.
Just then, he ripped out the plug.

"Don't take me!" cried the clozapine.
"Don't take me!" cried the poison.
And the door of the house creaked open,
and the cellar door lilted and murmured,
and the garden gate groaned and yawned
and let a little noise in.

There, just outside his window,
lurked life like a cheap cartoon.
He shut the sash, locked it, and checked it,
and checked it all afternoon.

He lowered the blinds on that world,
no longer an agent of it,
but then, with one finger, pulled down a slat
and set his eye above it.

At first it was grimly amusing,
at last it was grimly grim,

to watch all those hunched, hurried people,
who made like they weren't watching him.

The neighbors were thinking out loud.
They knew he was no fucking good.
So he slumped on a stool in the corner
like a bad little snaggletooth should.

They called him a dirty pig, and laughed,
and said he shouldn't exist.
Sometimes they made a tsking sound,
or oinked at him, or hissed.

They hissed that he was to blame
for everything, and everyone knew it,
and that if he weren't such a pussy
he'd know what to do, and he'd do it.

He lay on his side on the rug
unable to move at all
except for his big right toe,
which dug and dug at the wall,
    which dug at the wall,
        which dug.

"Don't take me!" cried the clozapine.
"Don't take me!" cried the cure.
And they begged him to sew his mouth shut
just to make goddamn sure.

"Don't take me!" cried the clozapine.
"Don't take me!" cried the poison.
And the gate to the wicked city gaped,
and the gates of the temple screamed and screamed,
and the gates of the garden groaned and yawned,

and the gates of the ziggurat gabbled in grief
and sucked all life's sorrows and joys in.

His thoughts were advancing like wolves.
He lay still for an hour and a half,
then reared up onto his rickety legs
like a newborn calf.

Then rug
hall
stairs
porch
stoop
street
and the blacktop humanly warm
on the soles of his naked feet.

His walk was stiffened by fear,
but it took him where he was going,
into the terrible world
of children and daffodils growing,
and friendly people helloing,
and the Super out doing the mowing,
and the two old sisters out in wool sweaters with their wrinkled cheeks pinkly glowing,
and the pretty lady who would give birth to Christmas barely showing but showing,
and the policeman helping to keep the lazy afternoon traffic flowing,
and time itself slowing,
and none of them, none of them knowing

that an odious axis was forming,
that it would not be controlled,

that schemes were afoot, that a foot
was a thing for a jackboot to hold,

that the street was a movie set,
that it was not warm and sunny,
that a creditor was calling
who could not be paid with money,

that the world was a like a sliver
of iron held in the hand,
and his mind the lodestone above it
that made it stir or stand,

that the air was slowly changing
to a color they didn't know,
that he was a famous doctor
on a television show.

But what could he do? Even friends
would take these facts for lies,
and he couldn't tell who the enemies were,
though he felt the hot breath of their eyes,

so he kept his big mouth shut
and tried to play along,
and plowed down the street toward the coffeeshop
as if nothing at all were wrong.

He tried not to notice the numbers
painted on garbage cans.
He tried and he tried not to look
at the black unmarked sedans.

The coffeeshop smelled like coffee,
but it felt different inside.
A new waitress went by. She winked.
He kept his eyes open wide.

Everything screamed, "Run away!"
But he wasn't really there!
So he stood by the gumball machines
and smiled and tried not to stare.

"The power is yours!" said a T-shirt.
"Look for lightning!" reported the weather.
And the stranger who offered the Sports section said,
"It's all there, Chief. Just put it together."

Then wild-eyed out of the kitchen
stormed a small, hard old man,
shouting in a strange language
and waving a frying pan,

shoving him out the door,
and into the chattering street,
shoving him, waving, shouting,
and pointing at his feet,
  at his bare, gray feet.

Then came the dark-blue uniform,
the badge glinting in the sun,
and the belt jangling like a storm trooper's
as the boots broke into a run.

"Take that!" cried the patrolman.
"Take that!" cried Johnny Law.
Street, knee, neck—
cuffs, curb, jaw.

And the flatfoot pushed him, bleeding,
into the sleek cruiser,
and he heard all the gawkers thinking
that he was a pig and a loser,

and his chin throbbed,
and the handcuffs ate at his wrist,
and he would be hacked into pieces soon
and would not be missed.

"Don't take me!" cried the victim.
"Don't take me!" cried the threat.
But the angry back of a head
was the only response he could get.

Lying on his side like a child
at the end of a big day,
he gazed up through the window
and watched it all slip away.

The little pen where they put him
had a toilet but no stall.
Here and there a message
scarred the gloss-white wall.

Time passed. But you couldn't tell it
on the trapped fly ticking the ceiling,
or the flickering light overhead,
or the sore on his chin congealing,
or on the sound of the other pigs in the other pens, squealing.

When the men came, he was ready.
He talked. They took it all down.

And soon they were back in the cruiser,
on their way across town.

Then, into the mirrored building,
over the waxed lobby floors,
down miles of echoing hallways,
through the heavy brown doors,

into a humming beige room
with a bed and a river view,
and an outside lock, and jailers
who wore white instead of blue.

"Take that," smiled the doctor.
"Take that," smiled the nurse.
He pressed his lips still tighter,
and things got worse and worse.

"Please!" threatened the nurse.
"Please!" growled the doctor.
He raised his fists to cover his mouth,
but the nurse was too close, and he clocked her.

Now into the room came the big man,
who did not clamor or shout,
but pinned him with ease to the bed,
strapped him down, and went out.

And the doctor was there again, trailing
a spiderweb of cologne,
and the doctor told what would happen next,
in an expert monotone,

and the nurse took a needle
and emptied it into his arm,
and they both left, content
that he could do no more harm,

and he fought, and the straps cut his shoulders,
and he gnawed at his lip, and it bled,
and he held his bladder for three long hours,
then shivered and pissed the bed.

When the doctor came a fifth time,
it was long past dawn.
They'd found him a room, said the doctor,
gently restraining a yawn.

The next two days were sleep,
and words through a fine white mist.
Then he woke inside a machine
whose motion he couldn't resist:

"Tick-tock," said the clock.
"Creak, creak," said the bed.
"Drip, drip," said the sink.
"Throb, throb," went his head.
"Ho-hum," sighed the night nurse.
"Heh, heh," said the sicko.
"Why? Why?" screamed the patient.
"Howl, howl!" cried the psycho.
"Wolf! Wolf!" cried the boy.
"Gobble, gobble!" sang the freaks.
"Sa, sa!" cried the king.
"Tick-tock," went the weeks.
"Bang, bang," said the TV.
"Teeter-totter," went his brain.

"Click, click," went the checkers.
"Pitter-patter," went the rain.
"Bring, bring," said the pay phone.
"Snip, snip," went Fate.
"Jangle, jingle," went the keys.
"Clank, clink," went the gate.
"Bye-bye," said the nurse.
"Bye-bye," said the guard.
"Bar-bar," said the doctor.
"Baa, baa," said the lamb.
"My, my," said his mother.
"Boohoo!" cried Bo Peep.
"Bowwow," said the wolf.
"Baa, baa," said the sheep.

In the car away from that place,
the family had a pleasant chat.
He seemed fine again, and humble,
though his speech was oddly flat.

He said that the halfway house
where he would be residing
was located on a quiet block and had
green vinyl siding.

There, he met new people
and watched the television,
which did not watch him back
or speak to him with derision,

and he performed certain tasks
meant to teach certain skills,
and he got small checks from the government
to pay his enormous bills.

Each night he fell asleep,
and each morning he got up,
and he washed down his medicine
and squashed the paper cup,

feeling, in all, much better,
more in touch with common sense,
and also slightly bored
by the lack of consequence.

And the church bells rang
and a dinner bell tinkled
and the school bell tolled
and called all the good girls and boys in.
And all of them brought all their toys in.
And all of them swallowed their poison.

James Matthew Wilson (b. 1975)

James Matthew Wilson's most recent book of poetry is *Saint Thomas and the Forbidden Birds* (Word on Fire, 2024). For more than two decades, he has distinguished himself as a poet of great moral seriousness, one who is utterly at home in formal verse traditions and has availed of them to mimic intricate patterns of thought, speech, and revelation. He is also a daring scholar and critic, having authored such volumes as *T. S. Eliot: Culture and Anarchy* (Wiseblood Books, 2024), *Catholic Modernism and the Irish "Avant-Garde"* (Catholic University of America Press, 2024), and *The Vision of the Soul: Truth, Beauty, and Goodness in the Western Tradition* (Catholic University of America Press, 2017).

Wilson is the Cullen Foundation Chair in English literature and the founding director of the MFA program in creative writing at the University of Saint Thomas in Houston, Texas. He has received prizes from the Catholic Media Awards, the Dallas Institute of Humanities, Memoria College, and the Conference on Christianity and Literature. Born in East Lansing, Michigan, he earned his undergraduate degree from the University of Michigan, a master's from the University of Massachusetts, and an MFA and PhD from the University of Notre Dame. He serves as poet-in-residence at the Benedict XIV Institute, scholar-in-residence of Aquinas College, and poetry editor of *Modern Age*. He is also editor of the Colosseum Books imprint of the Franciscan University Press, publisher of the present anthology.

BRIGHT APPLES

On this particular morning, the garage
Had donuts set out near the urn of coffee;
Brought by the boss, the secretary told me,
From an old cider mill on the west edge
Of Chester County. She had more to say,
About his generosity and how
I ought to take my children—if I had them—
Out there, when autumn came. The leaves would turn
And golden red would come to apple flesh
And drive their ripe weight down into the clay.
The deer would come as well, to crop the fruit,
Fattening themselves against the snow's long burial.
It seemed like a descent into nostalgia
To think of this, so hot the summer was,
As if the future were all burning pavement.
The heavy woman sitting next to me
Had one thick leg propped out—a broken femur,
She said, and rubbed her cane against the black
Boot she still wore, because it hadn't healed
All these months on. I tried to show my sympathy
With a grave nod, but that was not enough
For her. She levered on her stilt, then shuffled
Up to the secretary at her desk.
Settling her weight upon the cane's head, she
Explained that with the inquiry she'd lost
Her job, and now was caring for her mother,
Whose emphysema meant she had to stay
In bed, hooked up to oxygen. Near the end,
I guessed, and stared down at my open book.
They were descendants of George Washington,
The woman added, as if to explain

To the still-smiling secretary and
Anyone who would hear—which in effect
Meant me—how far they'd fallen in their sorrows.
Now, here she was, her Chrysler on the rack,
Waiting all morning just to hear what's wrong.
"They'll let you know just soon as they find out,"
Promised the secretary, and I wondered,
Did she believe the stories people told her
Or smile through them till she punched the clock,
The words of strangers, children, donuts, all
So many little details falling and gone.
The air was streaked with heat against the glassy
Front of the shop, gleaming in summer's climax.
From a blue door, propped open near the back,
Came the ring of a wrench being let to drop
Against the concrete floor, and a hydraulic
Lift humming as its load at last descended.

THE GREAT STATE OF ALASKA

When we signed up to take a weeklong cruise,
Docking in scenic ports along the coast of
The Great State of Alaska, our friends cooed.
Their voice betrayed that kind of awe and envy
Which skips ahead a few weeks to the future,
Postpones and puts far out of mind the vision
Of hosts of angels in their fearsome brilliance
Descending, with their swords out, at the world's end.
It clears a place in thought to feel warm water
Lapping against one's slick, recumbent shoulders;
To sense a grip, both firm and gentle, as
The manicurist pares one's nails and smooths
Fingers grown stubbed and raw in winter air.
One's cheeks grow pink and young in such a thought.
"You're going to *love* it," my friend Baxter said.
"Maybe you'll see a bear. *You'll* see a bear,"
He added, and then walked away, content,
Humming the same three notes in random sequence,
And vanished down the row of cubicles.
My wife's great aunt, a veteran in such matters,
Advised that we could keep aboard the ship,
Even in port, to savor the buffets.
"That's when you get the best of it," she said.
"They have to carve as much beef as you want."
From where we stood on deck, the world rose up
Above us with the sweep of granite bowls,
Trees at the base, which spread as thick as moss,
Then thinned until the weathered crown stood bare,
Pockmarked with remnants of the ancient snows.
The dome above us, gray and strained with clouds,
Hung like a marble tablet that had cracked.

Old women, traveling without their husbands,
Smiled at us as if we were newlyweds.
During the banquet, as the ship left port,
One placed a hand of cool, soft, paper-thin
Flesh on my own and begged us, love each other,
As her third husband loved her, till the end.
My wife's eyes glistened, as if very moved.
I looked down at the woman's rings and nodded.
We lived from meal to meal and each was long
And stuffing, the cuisine a far-flung hodgepodge
Of Thai, bread pudding, marinara sauce,
Great pork loins shaved beneath the orangey heat lamps,
And every seat, repose for those who'd come
For something so enduring it had sought
A stronghold here among the glacial bluffs.
Man's every urge, no matter how unlikely,
Including even the impossible
Desire to be thought wise regarding love,
Must somehow find its final refuge there.
One morning, with the ship drawn into shore,
And mist still hovering where the mountains' backs
Like great indifferent beasts passed one another,
We trailed our fellow tourists down the dock
And headed inland toward the Mendenhall,
With various promised stops along the way.
The promises of one remain with me.
The bus was crowded, quiet, save for coughs
That shook some septuagenarian
Out of his upright snooze. The gravelly roads
Lulled everyone toward sleep and my wife's head
Grew heavy on my shoulder, as we snaked
Around the bases of the coastal range,
Then up. The tired engine groaned and groaned,
Then stopped beneath a sky of towering firs.

The driver sat there, as if lost, until
A man named Caleb bounded up the steps
And stirred us with his scratchy, shouting voice
To come, to follow him, at last descend,
Into a clearing. Back behind him lay
A massive greenhouse; all about us, posted
In earth like pillars, stood inverted trunks
Of spruce and hemlock, fluted bowls pitched upward,
And where, once, long ago, the roots had clutched,
Now overflowed the cheery, pied strands
Of wildflowers, blessed, dangling in the breeze.
"It was no more than fifteen years ago,"
Caleb began, "A man the world now knows
As Ray came here and stood in this same plot.
The land about him was a waste and void.
The mountainside stood on the very brink,
One deluge more, of sliding out to sea,
Carrying with it what few broken stumps
And ruins from an old prospector's camp
Lay moldering about the steep terrain.
Mounting his excavator, Ray began to lodge
Into the dirt the trunks that had been felled.
He jammed their tops to earthward, plunged them deep,
And then, a lumberjack, he scaled those trunks,
And tossed into the elevated bowls
The seeds of every flower native here,
Till from such wreckage he had built this temple,
This place of florid beauty where we stand."
Caleb stood silent, overwhelmed with awe,
And watched the odd-ways grandeur sinking in.
He was not done, but led us, rather, up
The ribbon of a trail through woods infested
With devil's club, with trees that rose up from

The soft, moss-coated, rotting humps of trunks,
Whose opened bark spilled out their nourishing guts.
It was a brilliant darkness, lush with life
Fed off of life, the slow stir of the air
Carrying the drift of salt in from the sea,
And punctuated by the scents of *rosa*
Rugosa and delphiniums that grew
Wherever sunlight reached the sloping floor.
"Ray saved my life," our guide continued, "was
A second chance when I'd been lost and wandering.
He said, 'Your heart's broke, but you've got strong hands.'"
Tammy, Ray's wife, had done the same for others,
Apparently, and everyone who worked
The gardens owed their happiness to them.
Two orphan Eskimos had found a home
At last. An aged stevedore now spent
His days in charge of shaping up the bonsai.
A troop of girls who lost their way up north
By mystery and tragedy had come
To dwell as dryads over leaf and bud.
Beneath us, we heard someone chopping wood,
A strange hymn floating round each hack, as if
The rhythm of the earth had found its voice,
And mended every wound with harmony.
At last, we came out on the mountain crest,
A broad pole shelter running near the cliff's edge,
And in the center of a gravel plain,
The black and smoldering remnants of a fire.
Again, he spoke. "Last night, beneath the stars,
The daughter Ray and Tammy gave the world
Was married here, and Ray performed the nuptials.
The drums, guitar, and dancing went till dawn.
I haven't slept myself, but most our staff

Is home this morning, or snuck off to nap
In one of those small hiker's lodges Ray
Constructed from the timber of old Juneau."
    The gravel bore the prints of faded feet,
I thought, and heard, or thought I heard, the sound
Of empty bottles juggled through the air
And laughter at some clownish jubilation,
As, in the spell of celebration, each
Whirled crowns of flowers in the vacancies.
    I stared, from high, down on the continent
That opened wide before us, and could see
The foot trails leading pilgrims from afar,
From all the settled tracks and spoiled cities,
To here, where Ray and Tammy promised hope.
    Aboard ship once again, the dining room
Was lit aglow with golden candelabras;
A string quartet swayed slowly back and forth
And threaded all the air with some baroque
Melody leading somewhere that escaped me.
Women with elegance turned here and there,
Making their way between the feasting tables,
In gowns of blue or black, their breasts encrusted
With diamonds multiplying light on light.
Waiters flowed from the kitchen like champagne,
Their trays weighed down by plates of duck or lobster.
And just beyond the fullness of our chatter,
We saw the crowded heads of children laughing,
As with his dapper hat and gloves and cane
A coy magician summoned doves from nowhere.
    But even then, our exultation ripe,
Amid the clank of silver knives, the music,
Our heads grown light and vaporous and aswim
With cold and potent daiquiris, I heard

The coughs begin. And, in the days ahead,
The ship begun to roll as it pushed out
Far into the Pacific, all land vanished,
We lay upon the twin beds in our stateroom,
A deep and bellowing whoop within our chests,
Our bodies, churning, pulled away from us,
As if a drain had opened deep inside them,
As if they'd lose themselves within the deep.

And, as I gripped the corner of my mattress,
I thought that, yes, the world may be a temple
That opens onto somewhere not itself,
Much as black water opens wide its doors
To take within itself the giant orcas
That leap, then twist and fall with straining backs.

But no grove in its belly was a saved land,
No peak forever shelters us from nausea,
No place so fortifies itself that all
Becomes an everlasting dance of moonlight.
The engines sluicing water far below us,
And drawing us indifferently along
From port to port and none the final one,
I slowly came to know, there was, in fact,
No Ray, no Tammy, nor had ever been.

Paisley Rekdal (b. 1979)

Paisley Rekdal's poem "Philomela," which first ran in *Narrative* magazine, was chosen by Dana Gioia for *The Best American Poetry 2018* anthology (Scribner Poetry/Simon & Schuster, 2018) and appeared a year later in *Nightingale* (Copper Canyon Press, 2019), a rewriting of myths from Ovid.

In that collection, "Philomela" is accompanied by a prose piece, "Nightingale: A Gloss," which describes an act of sexual violence that befell her during a hike in Scotland. The essay justifies the poem's omission of key parts of the original myth, as told by Ovid in his *Metamorphoses*: the rape of Philomela and the severing of her tongue, the ghastly revenge that is served up to the villain Tereus, and Philomela's transformation to a nightingale. "Such details would be unimaginable, I think," she writes, "not because a reader can't imagine them, but because I don't want to." Poetry, after all, "suggests, but rarely achieves, the redress we desire."

Born in Seattle, Rekdal earned a bachelor's degree from the University of Washington, a master's from the University of Toronto, and an MFA from the University of Michigan in Ann Arbor. A professor of English at the University of Utah, she served as the state's poet laureate from 2017 to 2022. Two of her poetry books, *Animal Eye* (University of Pittsburgh Press, 2012) and *Imaginary Vessels* (Copper Canyon Press, 2016), were finalists for the Kingsley Tufts Poetry Award. *West: A Translation* (Copper Canyon Press, 2023) braids poems and essays to commemorate the 150th anniversary of the first transcontinental railroad. *Intimate* (Tupelo Press, 2011) is similarly a hybrid work, fusing text and photography to compose a family memoir. Rekdal's straight-up prose books include *Appropriate: A Provocation* (W. W. Norton, 2021) and *The Night My Mother Met Bruce Lee* (Penguin Random House, 2000). In 2024, W. W. Norton published *Real Toads, Imaginary Gardens*, Rekdal's guide to "reading and writing poetry forensically."

PHILOMELA

Because her grandmother loved
the arts, her father said, she'd willed
the money to a distant cousin
working as a sculptor. A decision
made the month before she'd died
from cancer, which the young woman
cannot now believe was due
only to a brain tumor, having endured
the last, deliberate ways her grandmother asked
why she'd never married.
The cousin who inherited the money
showed her sculptures in a converted barn,
the only space large enough to contain
the seething shapes that seemed to flame
up from their pedestals
in precarious arcs. An audacity
of engineering the young woman
tried not to see as a reproach
when, curious, she visited:
how the sculptures made her feel
too earthbound, solid. At the gallery,
she stared a long while at what she thought
was a tree blasted by lightning,
but the more she looked, the more clearly
shapes emerged. There
were a man's hands gripping a slender figure
by the waist, the thin body writhing,
frozen in his arms. It was
a girl, she saw, with shredded
bark for breasts and dark charred wood
for legs, as if the limbs had been snatched
from a fire while burning.

Her twig hands raked
her captor's face. The young woman
could read no emotion on it,
however: the plank face
had been scraped clean; all the fear
and anger burned instead inside
their twisting bodies: she could see
the two there stuck at a point
of perfect hatred for each other: she
for his attack, he for her resistance,
perhaps the beauty he could not
stand in her, as her last date in college
had hissed, "You think
you're so fucking pretty," spitting it
into her face so that she'd had to turn
her cheek to wipe it, which was when
he'd grabbed her harm, pinning her—

Was this why her cousin had been chosen, to make
what she'd had no words for?
Persephone, the piece she stood
amazed before had been titled: the last,
unconscious gift of her grandmother.
"For your wedding," she'd said
her last week, pointing
to her own open palm in which
nothing rested. Perhaps
her grandmother had imagined
a gold ring there. Perhaps a string
of thick pink pearls. The young woman
drove home from the gallery, took a shower,
and did not tell anyone that day
what it was she'd seen. A month later,
in the mail, a package came

from her father: her grandmother's Singer
sewing machine, its antique brass wheel
scrubbed of gold, the wooden handle
glossy with vines of mother-of-pearl.
It was lovely, and for a moment
she considered sewing a quilt with it,
onto which she might embroider
shooting stars in reds and saffron, the figure
of a child, perhaps, out of a man
by a house's courtyard, his hat
in his hands, his broad body
naked, harmless.

How much thread would that take
to make? she wondered. And considered it
a long while before packing up
the machine again, sliding it back
into its wooden crate and high up onto a shelf
of her bedroom closet. The place she kept
some books, old clothes, and college papers,
where she told herself it could wait.

Isabella Hsu (b. 1996)

Born in Redondo Beach, California, Isabella Hsu is an MFA candidate in the creative writing program at the University of St. Thomas. She is the assistant executive editor at *Dappled Things*, a Catholic literary journal. Her poems and other writings have appeared in *St. Austin Review* and *San Diego Reader*. The title of her contribution refers to an episode from the Gospel of Luke, in which Jesus brings back to life the son of a widow in the city of Nain.

THE YOUNG MAN AT NAIN

Summoned from out of sleep, his eyes are opened
Against his will. A rolling wave of nausea
Forces them shut again. He must be on
His father's boat—of all his fears the fear
Of water is his greatest. Rising now,
He's startled at the sight of rooftops, waves
Are nowhere to be seen below. He strains
To orient himself and hears the sounds
Of lamentation or of prayer. Then some
Black form sweeps near, and memories begin
To stir. He sees a face, *her* face; the one
Which he has known through all his life. The bier
On which he lies is lowered now to touch
The earth. His mother presses close to him
To kiss his face, his hands, his trembling eyes—
This woman whom he failed to love in life.
Now all at once, he sees what is to come:
Unending days spent toiling for them both,
And always she'll be near to praise her son.

When first his father died, they grew together,
Two trees entwined, the widow and her son.
Behind the low walls of their house, with closed
Air weighing heavy, they placed stone on stone,
Each act of love a wall to keep the world
From breaking in, which never stopped to mourn.
But time wore down her touch, wore down his trust.
And growing sensitive to what exists
Between things: space and silence, he began
To dream of life without her constant touch
And close breath on his skin. He grew afraid:

Had she learned how to read his heart, its subtle
And silent movements? Could she know his sin?

The crowd has stopped and gathered now outside
The low stone wall and judgment seat. His life
Reveals itself in sudden clarity—
Despite his best attempts it will not stop
Or slow. The quiet certainty of fear
Begins to grow and he is powerless;
He knows he will not rest until she dies,
Knows the dull spinning of his life, a top
He can't control: once more to sin, unthinking;
Once more to drink too much; and he will gaze
At women, at the wives of other men.
From deep within this quiet rage, he'll hate
All that he can't possess. Perhaps there will
Be days where he will wake with hope for who
He might become. He will not shrink from her
Insistent touch, from all that love demands.
And for a while he will forget his hate
And how it doubles back upon itself
In times of peace. He will forget until
The morning that he wakes to find it waiting,
To indicate the objects of its lust:
Each movement that she makes, the rasping way
In which she breathes, her love, which kills his own.
When that day comes, he knows he will not fight
The truth he feels, a sinking stone within:
A fallen man will always fall again.

He's roused by joyous shouts, praise made to God,
Before him crowds have fallen to their knees.
He cannot hear their words above the sound
Of pulsing blood inside his ears. The thrill

Of fear and nausea courses through him and
The road begins to rise in violent waves.
His fingers seek his mother's hands; he clings
To them for strength. He wants to cry, to sob
Aloud—perhaps he does but he can't hear
His voice above the din. He cries just as
He did when he had watched his father's body
Borne out beyond the city's walls; he cries
Just as he cried when he was a young, on board
His father's boat for the first time. The fish,
Their writhing silver bodies like the sea,
Surrounded him; the sun and waves were blinding.
Crouched on his knees, he spent the day being sick.

His eyes blink open and he sees a face,
Upturned and gazing back at him. Amid
The crowd, this face stands out; its eyes are hard
And cold. His mind goes quiet and his heart
Beats louder than before. He hears his mother,
Her voice now young and carried on the wind.
He writhes, he fights, his body won't obey.
He longs to run back to his home. And now
The shore, the waves—they rise like a reprieve.
If only he could move enough to kneel.
If only he could move enough to beg.
If everyone were silent, he'd cry out
His only prayer: *take back what you have done.*
Have mercy not on her but on her son.

Acknowledgments

"Barn Siding" and "The Purpose of Poetry" from *After the Rain* by Jared Carter, © 1993, reprinted by permission of the author. "Signifyin' Monkey" and "Black Ice and Rain" from *Collected Poems*, © 2009 by Michael Donaghy. Reproduced by permission of the Licensor through PLSclear. "The Bistro Styx," from *Mother Love*, © 1995 by Rita Dove. Used by permission of W. W. Norton & Company, Inc. "Seven Curses," words and music by Bob Dylan, © 1967 Universal Tunes. Copyright renewed. All rights reserved. Used by permission. Reprinted by permission of Hal Leonard, LLC. "Lily, Rosemary and the Jack of Hearts," words and music by Bob Dylan, © 1975 Universal Tunes. Copyright renewed. All rights reserved. Used by permission. Reprinted by permission of Hal Leonard, LLC.

"The Ferryman" and "Helen" from *The Boy in the Well: And Other Poems*, © 1995 by Daniel Mark Epstein. Reprinted by permission of the author. "Les Passages," from *Usher: Poems*, © 2009 by B. H. Fairchild. Used by permission of W. W. Norton & Company, Inc. "Counting the Children," "Haunted," and "The Ballad of Jesus Ortiz" from *99 Poems: New and Selected*, © 2017 by Dana Gioia. Reprinted by permission of The Permissions Company, LLC on behalf of Graywolf Press, Minneapolis, Minnesota, www.graywolfpress.org. "Vendanges" from *Desperanto: Poems 1999–2002*, © 2003 by Marilyn Hacker. Used by permission of W. W. Norton & Company, Inc. "Dickens on Fire" from *Sometimes I Dream That I Am Not Walt Whitman*, © 2020 by Joseph Harrison. Reprinted by permission of Waywiser Press. "The Young Man at Nain" reprinted by permission of the author. "Inspectors" and "Walking Backward" from *Walking Backward*, © 1999 by Paul Lake. Reprinted by permission of the Estate of Paul Lake. "The Feud" from *To the Bone: New and Selected Poems*, © 1996 by Sydney Lea. Used by permission of University of Illinois Press. "Passages from Friday" and "Coda: Mr. Dorrington's Discovery" from *Starting from Sleep: New and Selected Poems*, © 2022 by Charles Martin. Reprinted by permission of the author. "Spooning," "Gusev," and "The Collector's Tale" from *The Sound: New and Selected Poems*, © 2018 by David Mason. Reprinted by permission of The Permissions Company, LLC on behalf of Red Hen Press, redhen.org. "The Dream Job" and "The Orange Bottle" from *Accepting the Disaster*, © 2014 by Joshua Mehigan. Reprinted by permission of Farrar, Straus and Giroux. All rights reserved. "Freeman Field" and "The Ballad of Aunt Geneva" from *The Fields of Praise: New and Selected Poems*, Louisiana State University Press, 1997. "Philomela" from *Nightingale*, © 2019 by Paisley Rekdal. Reprinted with the permission of The Permissions Company, LLC on behalf of Copper Canyon Press, coppercanyonpress.org. "True Story of the Pins" from *Whispering to Fool the Wind*, © 1982 by Alberto Rios. Reprinted by permission of Sheep Meadow Press. "First Words" from *The Lime Orchard Woman: Poems*, © 1988 by Alberto Rios. Reprinted by permission of Sheep Meadow Press. "Refugio's Hair" from *The Smallest Muscle in the Human Body*, © 2002 by Alberto Rios. Reprinted by permission of The Permissions Company, LLC on behalf of Copper Canyon Press, coppercanyonpress.org. "Frost at Midnight" from *Sunday Skaters*, © 1994 by Mary Jo Salter. Used by permission of Alfred A. Knopf, an imprint of the Knopf Doubleday Publishing Group, a division of Penguin Random House, LLC. "Two Tales of Clumsy" and "Darwin in 1881" from *Supernatural Love: Poems 1976–1992*, © 2000 by Gjertrud Schnackenberg. Reprinted by permission of Farrar, Straus and Giroux. All rights reserved. "Birth of a Critical Spirit" from *Comforting the Wilderness*, © 1977 by Robert B. Shaw. Published by Wesleyan University Press, Middletown, Connecticut. Used by permission of Wesleyan University Press. "Hide-and-Seek" from *What Remains to Be Said*, © 2022 by Robert B. Shaw. Reprinted by permission of Pinyon Publishing. "Ethel's Sestina" and "Siblings" are used by permission from *Blood Dazzler* (Coffee House Press), © 2008 by Patricia Smith. "Battle of Plataea" and "Lost and Found" from *Like: Poems*, © 2018 by A. E. Stallings. Reprinted by permission of Farrar, Straus and Giroux. All rights reserved. "February 18, 1943" from *Keeping My Name*, © 2006 by Catherine Tufariello. Reprinted by permission of Texas Tech University Press. "Madeleine for a While" from *Sakura Park*, © 2006 by Rachel Wetzsteon. Reprinted by permission of Persea Books, Inc. (New York), www.perseabooks.com. All rights reserved. "Bright Apples" from *The Hanging God*, © 2008 by James Matthew Wilson. Reprinted by permission of Angelico Press. "The Great State of Alaska" from *Saint Thomas and the Forbidden Birds*, © 2024 by James Matthew Wilson. Reprinted by permission of Words on Fire. "The Ice Storm" from *Hard Night*, © 2005 by Christian Wiman. Reprinted by permission of The Permissions Company, LLC on behalf of Copper Canyon Press, coppercanyonpress.org. "Dirty Dan" and "Tomorrow & Tomorrow" from *More Things in Heaven: New and Selected Poems*, © 2022 by David Yezzi. Reprinted by permission of Measure Press.

The editor would like to extend special thanks to James Matthew Wilson and Dana Gioia for their support, confidence, and advice; to Sarah Wear and Taylor Caputo at Franciscan University Press for their kindness, forbearance, and the payment and processing of permission fees; to Ashleigh McKown for her meticulous care as copy editor; and to the following people and institutions for granting permission to reprint poems for free: Rachel Lake, Charles Martin, Coffee House Press, Texas Tech University Press, Waywiser Press, Angelico Press, and Words on Fire.

Index of Titles

"Barn Siding," 2
"Battle of Plataea: Aftermath," 230
"Birth of a Critical Spirit," 83
"Black Ice and Rain," 94
"Bright Apples," 262

"Coda: Mr. Dorrington's Discovery," 51
"Counting the Children," 99

"Darwin in 1881," 144
"Dickens on Fire," 179
"Dirty Dan," 190

"Ethel's Sestina," 175

"February 18, 1943," 187
"First Words," 136
"Freeman Field," 79
"Frost at Midnight," 150

"Gusev," 157

"Haunted," 106
"Helen," 90
"Hide-and-Seek," 85

"Inspectors," 120

"Les Passages," 54
"Lily, Rosemary and the Jack of Hearts," 25
"Lost and Found," 233

"Madeleine for a While," 227

"Passages from Friday," 30
"Philomela," 271

"Refugio's Hair," 137

"Seven Curses," 23
"Siblings," 177
"Signifyin' Monkey," 92
"Spooning," 159

"The Ballad of Aunt Geneva," 77
"The Ballad of Jesús Ortiz," 114
"The Bistro Styx," 130
"The Collector's Tale," 165
"The Dream Job," 247
"The Ferryman," 88
"The Feud," 61
"The Great State of Alaska," 264
"The Ice Storm," 209
"The Orange Bottle," 248
"The Pig Roast," 246
"The Purpose of Poetry," 21
"The Young Man at Nain," 275
"Tomorrow & Tomorrow," 194
"True Story of the Pins," 134
"Two Tales of Clumsy," 140

"Vendages," 56

"Walking Backward," 124

Index of Poets

Carter, Jared, 1
"Barn Siding," 2
"The Purpose of Poetry," 21

Donaghy, Michael, 91
"Signifyin' Monkey," 92
"Black Ice and Rain," 94
Dove, Rita, 129
"The Bistro Styx," 130
Dylan, Bob, 22
"Lily, Rosemary and the Jack of Hearts," 23
"Seven Curses," 25

Epstein, Daniel Mark, 87
"The Ferryman," 88
"Helen," 90

Fairchild, B. H., 53
"Les Passages," 54

Gioia, Dana, 98
"Counting the Children," 99
"Haunted," 106
"The Ballad of Jesús Ortiz," 114

Hacker, Marilyn, 55
"Vendanges," 56
Harrison, Joseph, 178
"Dickens on Fire," 179
Hsu, Isabella, 274
"The Young Man at Nain," 275

Lake, Paul, 119
"Inspectors," 120
"Walking Backward," 124
Lea, Sydney, 60
"The Feud," 61

Martin, Charles, 29
"Passages from Friday," 30
"Coda: Mr. Dorrington's Discovery," 51
Mason, David, 156
"Gusev," 157
"Spooning," 159
"The Collector's Tale," 165
Mehigan, Joshua, 245
"The Pig Roast," 246
"The Dream Job," 247
"The Orange Bottle," 248

Nelson, Marilyn, 76
"Freeman Field," 77
"The Ballad of Aunt Geneva," 79

Rekdal, Paisley, 270
"Philomela," 271
Rios, Alberto, 133
"True Story of the Pins," 134
"First Words," 136
"Refugio's Hair," 137

Salter, Mary Jo, 149
"Frost at Midnight," 150

Schnackenberg, Gjertrud, 139
"Two Tales of Clumsy," 140
"Darwin in 1881," 144
Shaw, Robert B., 82
"Birth of a Critical Spirit," 83
"Hide-and-Seek," 85
Smith, Patricia, 174
"Ethel's Sestina," 175
"Siblings," 177
Stallings, A. E., 229
"Battle of Plataea: Aftermath," 230
"Lost and Found," 233

Tufariello, Catherine, 186
"February 18, 1943," 187

Wetzsteon, Rachel, 226
"Madeleine for a While," 227
Wilson, James Matthew, 261
"Bright Apples," 262
"The Great State of Alaska," 264
Wiman, Christian, 208
"The Ice Storm," 209

Yezzi, David, 189
"Dirty Dan," 190
"Tomorrow & Tomorrow," 194